Clinch Fighting for Mixed Martial Arts

Clinch Fighting for Mixed Martial Arts

MIKE SWAIN & CHUCK JEFFERSON

EMPIRE Books

P.O. Box 491788, Los Angeles, CA 90049

First published in 2006 by Empire Books

First edition
06 05 04 03 02 01 00 99 98 97 1 3 5 7 9 10 8 6 4 2

Empire Books
P.O. Box 491788
Los Angeles, CA 90049

Printed in the United States of America.

Library of Congress: 2006009378
ISBN-10: 1-933901-07-1
ISBN-13: 978-1-933901-07-7

Library of Congress Cataloging-in-Publication Data

Swain, Mike, 1960-
   Clinch fighting for mixed martial arts / by Mike Swain and Chuck Jefferson. -- 1st ed.
      p. cm.
   Includes index.
   ISBN 1-933901-07-1 (pbk. : alk. paper)
   1. Hand-to-hand fighting. 2. Martial arts. I. Jefferson, Chuck, 1976-
II. Title.
   GV1111.S93 2006
   796.81--dc22
                                        2006009378

Dedication

We dedicate this book to our mutual coach, mentor and good friend Sensei Yoshihiro Uchida founder and head Judo coach of San Jose State University. Through his persistent teachings, thousands of students have successfully graduated with stronger minds and characters to live life to its fullest.

Acknowledgements

The creation of this book has been very much a team effort since the authors conceived it in 2005.

To David Torres, for his assistance in the photographic sessions. Your help and dedication is truly appreciated.

To Jim Nagareda, photographer, who put in many hours in front of the camera capturing all the technical details.

To Wallid Ismail [Jungle Fight], who provided wonderful photographs to illustrate the book as well.

Table of Contents

About the Authors

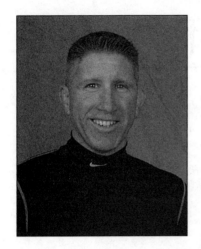

MIKE SWAIN

Mike Swain, a business marketing graduate from San Jose State University, is president and CEO of Swain Sports International.

The name Mike Swain has become synonymous with judo worldwide. Swain made history in 1987 by becoming the first male World Champion from the western hemisphere. In addition, Mike has won a medal in all major international tournaments, including the Olympics (1988 bronze), World Championships (1985 silver, 1987 gold, 1989 silver), and Pan American Games (1987 gold). He is a four-time Olympian, five-time World Team member, and was the 1996 U.S. Olympic judo coach for the Atlanta Games.

To hone his skills during his competitive career, Mike frequently traveled to Japan, where he trained relentlessly. While there, he trained at Nihon University, one of Japan's top Judo Universities, as well as with the Tokyo Police Academy.

In addition to his many awards, in 1985 Mike was honored as Black Belt Magazine's "Competitor of the Year" and in 1995 as "Instructor of the Year." Recently, Mike received the prestigious "Titan Award" from the U.S. Olympic Committee as the pioneer for USA Judo. Other Titan recipients include Evander Holyfield for boxing and Dan Gable for wrestling.

Mike also was co-producer of several martial art TV shows: Pro Judo, Pro Tae Kwon Do, and Sumo, which all have premiered on ESPN or ESPN2. In demand as a teacher, coach and seminar leader, Swain also is involved in market development for Century Martial Arts. His knowledge of grappling and clinch techniques is unsurpassed, making him one of the most sought-after submission teachers in the field.

CHUCK JEFFERSON

Chuck Jefferson was raised in Barstow, California and began his judo training under Coach Ernie Smith at the age of 5. Throughout his youth and early teens, Chuck compiled close to twenty junior national medals and attended training camps in the former Soviet Union. At age 18, Chuck moved on to train with the legendary judo team at San Jose State University under coach Yosh Uchida.

During his college career, Chuck dominated his weight class at the Collegiate National Championships, winning the tournament 4 years in a row. He also represented the United States at the World University Championships in 1996 & 1998. During this time, Chuck also trained at Tokai University in Japan, a school renowned for producing multiple Olympians and World Champions.

After graduating college, Chuck began to focus all of his time and energy on Judo. He continued to train at Tokai University during the off season and started attending tournaments and training camps across Europe. Chuck went on to win the Pan American Championships in both 2002 and 2003. He also represented the United States at the 2003 World Championships in Osaka, Japan.

With multiple national championships and gold medals at most major tournaments in the Western Hemisphere, Chuck has become one of the top judo competitors in the United States. He is a Certified Strength and Conditioning Specialist (CSCS) with the National Strength and Conditioning Association and currently spends his time coaching and training the judo team at San Jose State University.

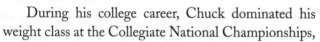

Introduction

By Jose Fraguas

There is no doubt Mixed Martial Arts (MMA) has revolutionized the world of sport combat. Since the appearance in 1993 of the Ultimate Fighting Championship, the concept of mixing elements from different martial arts and combat systems has taken the sport to a new level.

Based on the reality of MMA, some technical elements have been developed that parallel the evolution of the sport. First, it was the "guard," popularized by three-time UFC champion Royce Gracie. Then, when fighters learned how to defend against the unsophisticated methods of clos-ing the gap and getting into the clinch used by Brazilian fighters—who dominated the scene on the ground—it was the "takedowns" from wrestling that dominated the game. Wrestlers showed the world how to "shoot" for the opponent's legs and take him down in a split second. They [wrestlers] brought an important part of what today is known as the "MMA style."

The striking elements of punching and kicking were absorbed from Muay Thai Boxing and the European approach to kickboxing. The use of the knees and elbows also was borrowed from the lethal art of Muay Thai. With the "shoot" technique and the techniques from Muay Thai and European kickboxing, the current MMA fighting package was beginning to take form.

But there has been a "missing link" in the development of this new approach [style] to the MMA, and that is the "clinch." Since the groundwork has a relevant part in the current MMA picture, it is logical that the previous stage of combat [clinch] has to be developed to fill the gap in the fighting format the sport was providing.

Due to the lack of gi use in MMA, the clinch aspect of combat has been reduced to a simple "close-in position between the fighters, each trying to unbalance the other with little sophistication and technical knowledge of the circumstances." There is no doubt that "clinch fighting," or the "standing clinch," is one of the most misunderstood elements of MMA today.

It is the "opening door" to groundwork as soon as one of the fighters blocks or intercepts the opponent's attempt to take him down. The use of the fence in the cage offers a wide spectrum of possibilities to be used, but the fundamental techniques and skills should be learned beforehand.

The clinch, as used in MMA today, is a combination of Greco-Roman wrestling, Judo, Jiu Jitsu and Thai Boxing. Elements from these styles are properly modified, combined, and adapted to fit the format of the sport.

The two most important points to have in mind when fighting in a clinch position are: a) if the clinching is done properly, there is very little chance of getting hurt by any strike of your opponent; and b) you can easily throw the opponent onto the ground without losing control of the situation.

The elements from wrestling and the no-Gi Judo are used mainly to control the opponent in the standing clinch, while modified Judo throws and leg trips, together with wrestling slamming techniques like the *suplex,* are the perfect combination for this range of combat.

In this book, we are going to study and analyze the grappling elements of Clinch Fighting without incorporating the striking aspects of the elbows and knees. It basically deals with the specific elements of the Clinch. Only when you have already mastered certain aspects of the clinch, such as the tie-ups, hand and body positions, hooks and throws, should you incorporate the striking element into the equation. Take the study of clinch fighting one step at a time. Create a solid foundation in body feel and skill from the grappling arts, and then add the elbows and knees to it. The fighter with a superior knowledge of the "clinch" has a

tremendous advantage in any MMA contest.

The throwing aspects of clinch fighting have become the center point of study in MMA. Randy Couture, the great UFC champion, is a true example of how to combine elements from different grappling arts into a solid technical structure that allows him to throw any opponent to the ground.

Clinch fighting is a very powerful tool in the MMA fighter's arsenal. It is the position from where he will move into a more dominant position—most likely on the ground. It is not a position from where the fighter can actually use submission techniques, but a *transitional* position that opens the door for a resolving move.

Remember that all throws from a clinch position are based on the natural laws of physics, and a good MMA fighter always relies on angular momentum. The concept of a circle should be combined with the principles of mechanical leverage in all controlling and throwing techniques.

There are some important tips to remember when finding yourself in a clinch fighting position:

- Keep your body close to your opponent's. Otherwise, you'll be in serious danger of being hit with knees to the stomach and elbows to the face.

- Use your hip to "feel" the opponent's body, and angle your trunk in a search for a dominant position.

- When holding your opponent's head, always keep your elbows in to gain a better control position.

- Be aware of the knee strike to the inside and outside parts of your legs. These can be very damaging if properly applied.

- Keep your head looking sideways. Don't offer your full frontal face to your opponent.

- First, protect yourself. Then, attack the opponent.

- Double overhooks are a dominant position. Don't let your opponent catch you with this technique. Your arms will be trapped and your options will be very limited.

- Try to throw your opponent by a quick and harmonious action of the body. This requires long training for good form and proper timing.

- Plan to execute attacks by combinations. Continuous attacks can only be brought successfully if the fighter attacks earnestly with the first technique. Most people don't make the first attack with enough impetus; consequently, they do not get the proper reaction and fail in the second.

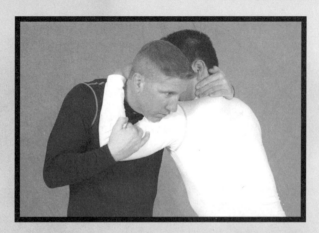

HOLDS & STANCES

The definition of clinch is to grapple at close quarters so as to be closely engaged. Therefore, there are many variations that can be defined as a clinch. Here are some basic holds of the clinch, as well as a few stances for forward and backward body positions for throws.

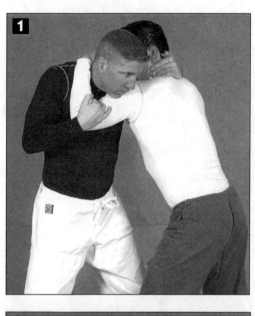
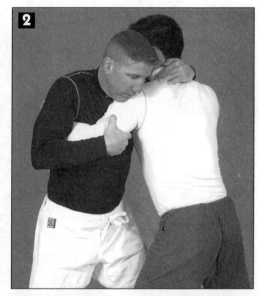

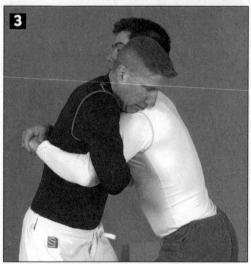
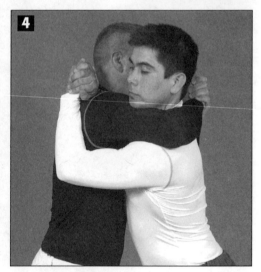

Clinch Holds

Here are some basic Clinches or holds, which are referential points of attack. The most important thing about these holds is to have a firm grip with both hands on some body part such as the neck, arm, shoulder, or wrist, in order to off-balance your opponent. Knowing when to attack comes from experience and reading when your opponent's body is off balance in a split second. (1) This is in a basic head and elbow. 2) Head and arm. 3) Under–Over—both arms are locked around the opponent's upper arm, but your core is lowered to maintain balance. 4) Neck and arm, with the left arm under opponent's arm, cranking upwards to keep him off balance.

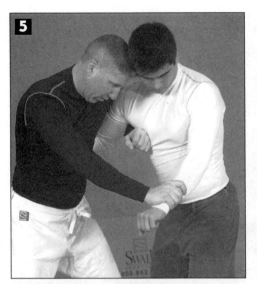

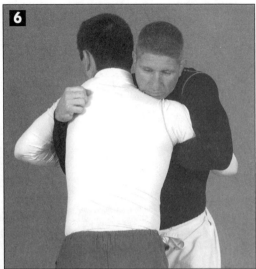

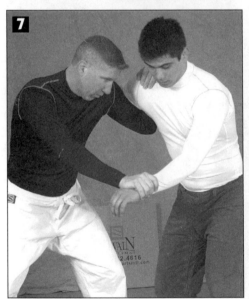

5) Over hook and wrist, sometimes called a wizard in wrestling. Again, the core or hips are lowered and away, to maintain balance for offensive and defensive movement. 6) Under hook and over hook. 7) Under hook and wrist. Keep your hand on opponent's shoulder for leverage. 8) Keep two hands on neck and your elbows in for defense and offense.

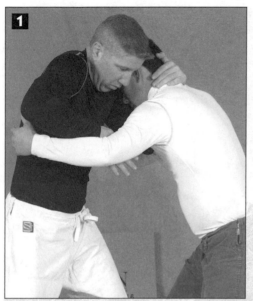

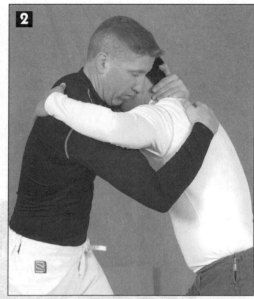

Fighting for position

Known in Greco-Roman wrestling as pummeling, both fighters try to get the better grip to initiate a throw or takedown. Often used in training as an exercise in which both fighters continue to jockey for position with under and over hook movements. Where you keep your core is very important; if you do not bend your knees and lower your body, you can be picked up and tossed in a second.

1–2) Begin to pry your right arm under your opponent's for better position. 3) Your opponent applies the same technique to reverse the position.

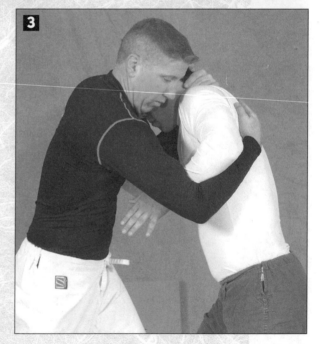

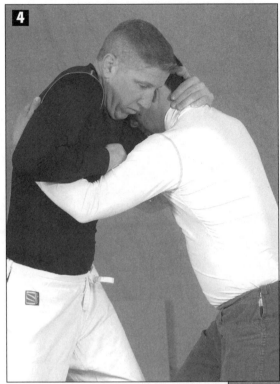

4–5) Back your hips out and lower your core again to gain position.

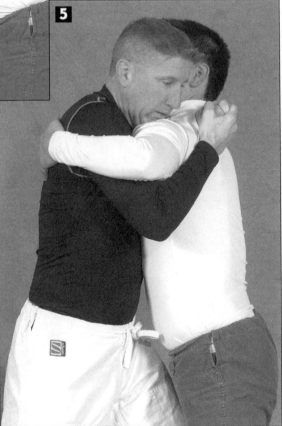

23

Body Positions
Throughout this book, you will see a variety of throws. Keep in mind there are three elements to all throws: a) Off-balancing; b) Position; and c) Following through or Finish. The following pictures refer to the second element, called "Position."

(1) **Side Body Drop.** Back straight, knees slightly bent, and feet a little wider than shoulders. The main object is to throw or drop your opponent off your pivoting foot, or to your side.

2) **Shoulder throw.** Back straight and knees bent in the direction of the throw.

3) **Inside foot trip.** The sweeping leg is straight, with the supporting leg bent for power. Your opponent is thrown straight back, not to the side.

4) **Inner thigh throw.** This throw takes good balance. Your supporting leg should be bent and the sweeping or upward leg as straight as possible. This throw is often used to counter a single leg takedown with a wizard and wrist.

LEG TRIP TAKEDOWNS

Leg trip takedowns are probably the safest attacks with no Gi or uniform. Using your footsweeps and hooks like a boxer uses his jab will keep your opponent off balance and set up many other finishing techniques. The key is to use your leg or foot as a guide for the takedown, and not the main element. The key is to off-balance your opponent in the clinch with movement, and then finish the takedown with the leg trip.

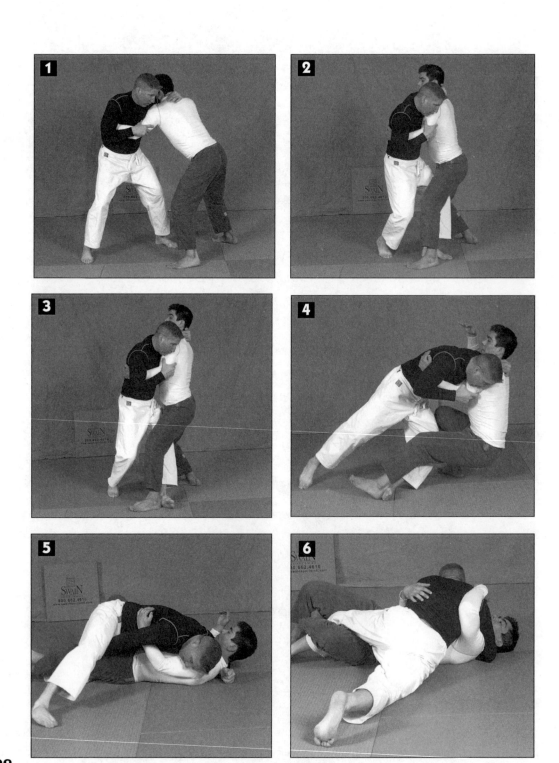

From the neck and arm clinch, pull your opponent's neck forward to create a reaction. 2) As the opponent stands up, lower your core and slide in like a fencer step, keeping tight. 3–4) Lunge forward, pushing off the back toe straight backward. 5) Control the upper body, leaving no space to move, while pushing down on the knee with your left hand to pass the leg. 6) Control the upper body with two arms.

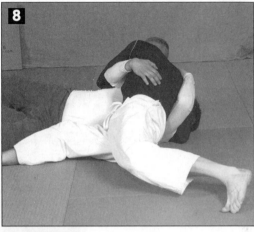

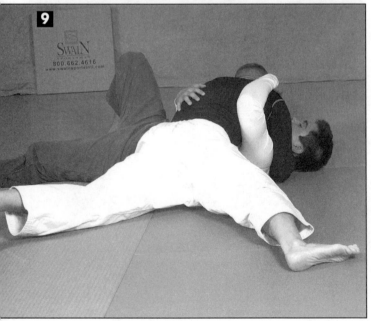

7) Using your toe on his upper leg, pry out the other leg. 8) Bring the escaping leg back quickly to protect from the bridge. 9) Spread your base for the hold or side mount control.

Starting from the neck and arm clinch, 2) lunge forward and pop your arm straight up under his chin to pick up the head, while simultaneously grabbing behind the knee. 3) It is important to pick up the leg without bending down too much.

4) Finish the throw by sweeping out the leg. This is a hard fall to take and should be quickly followed with passing his legs before they can gain guard control.

Starting from the under hook one hand, 2) move sideways and gain wrist control. 3) Nearly simultaneously, slide your forward foot in to sweep out the leading foot. The key here is to take the foot out in the direct his toes are pointing for less friction and resistance. 4) Stay close on the finish.

Bring your knee through to pass the leg. Then, switch your hips to secure side control while keeping your hip bone on top of his head or temple for maximum pressure.

33

1) Starting from the under hook wrist control clinch, 2) pop out his leg by stepping inside the ankle and raising the hook while pulling the wrist forward. 3) As the opponent pulls back, slide in chest to chest and reap the foot again in the direction of the toe. You can use the sole of your foot or your heel as in picture 3 to bring your body closer.

4) Stay close to eliminate space while pushing down on the knee to pass the legs. 5) Slide your left leg through for the side control or pin.

35

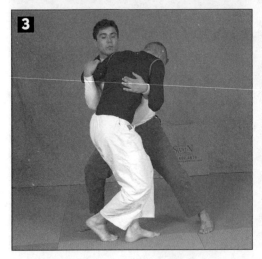

1. Starting from a neck and arm clinch.
2. Circle step to the right while pulling down on his neck.
3. As they pull back up, bring your trailing foot closer to push off.
4. Now drop your core and backsweep his ankle with you heel.
    Keep your weight on his arm that is around your body.

5. Follow down, eliminating any space.
6. Slide your leg through for the pin.

37

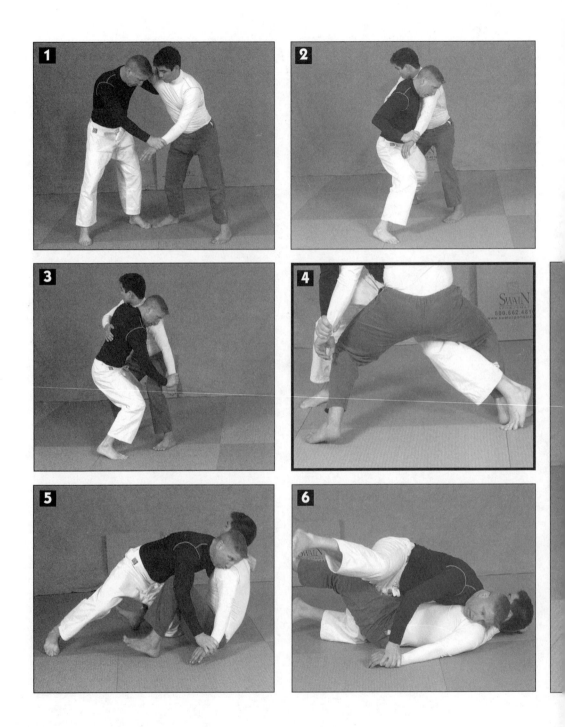

1. Starting from an under hook and wrist,
2. Hook the close ankle and take a step sideways.
3. Lower your core and push back the wrist.
4. Attack the leg with a wide sweep, pushing back.
5. Follow to the ground maintaining wrist control.
6. Pass the leg.
7. Control the upper half of the body.

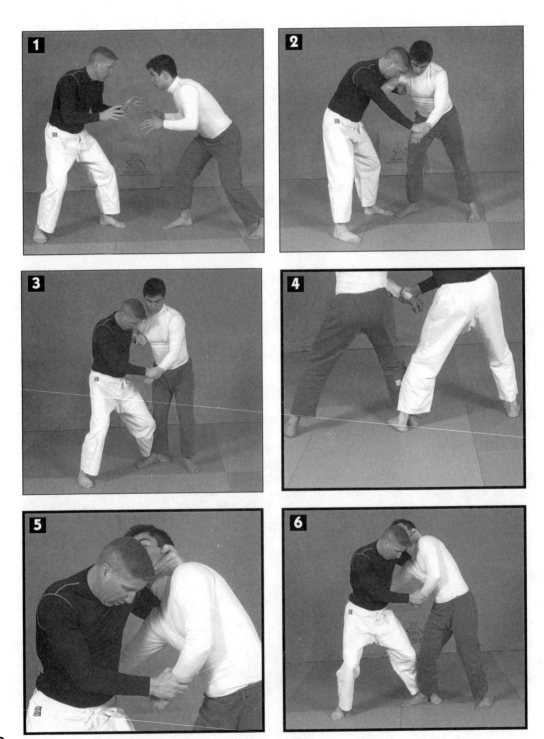

1. From an open position, no clinch,
2. Gain the over hook and wrist.
3. Slide your foot behind the ankle, keeping you shin in front of his shin to trap the leg.
4. A back view as opponent turns away to escape.
5. Cup the far neck for better head control.
6. Maintain the hook by keeping your foot stuck to his ankle.

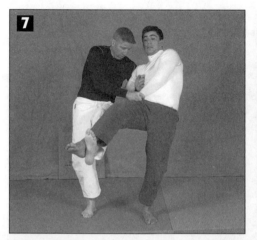

7. As opponent tries to lift his foot, lift up. Do not try to lift the foot when weight is posted.
8. Follow close to the ground.
9. Turn into opponent for the pin.

1. Starting from a stand up clinch,
2. Block knee strike with your elbow.

3. Grab knee and thrust upwards with other arm simultaneously.
4. Follow through, sweeping out the leg with your whole body.

Perhaps one of the best times to attack using small leg trips is against the cage, ring, or wall. Most fighters tend to lean away and relax. The key is to make them take small steps by repositioning your body.

1. I have a high clinch with control.
2. As I change my stance from right clinch to left clinch, my opponent steps forward with his left foot.
3. Lower your core and make the opponent feel your weight.

4. As you straighten up, so does your opponent, which creates the perfect time to sweep.
5. Maintain ground control once he goes down.
6. Elbow in the solar plexus.

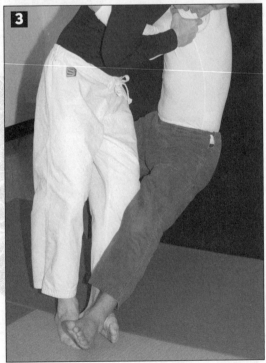

1. Starting from the right clinch,
2. Through the head to the side with your right hand.
3. Slide in left clinch, sweeping the foot at the same time.

4. Close up of sweeping foot
   position.
5. Eliminate space for ground
   control.

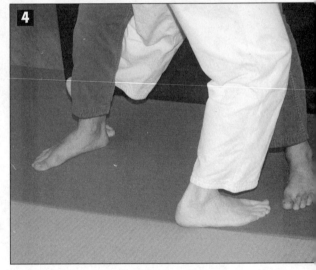

1. Starting from a clinch with opponent against the wall,
2. Lower you core and lean your weight across his body.
3. Sweep out the close leg in a semicircle direction at the base of the heel.
4. Close-up of the foot position.

5. Opponent should fall down and to the side.
6. Follow up quickly for ground control.

1. Now the clinch is reversed and your back is against the wall.
2. As opponent tries an outside leg reap, hook the ankle and make the same semicircle as before.
3. Move your body out away from the wall for the sweep.

4. The opponent's body should drop straight down, putting
   you in a good ground position.

1. Starting from a head and arm clinch,
2. Attack the far outside leg, hooking the back of the opponent's knee with your heel. Keep your chin down. As he blocks this attack by stepping his leg back,
3. Switch to the inside circle sweep and push forward off your back foot for power.
4. Finish the throw so his body falls straight back and not to the side.

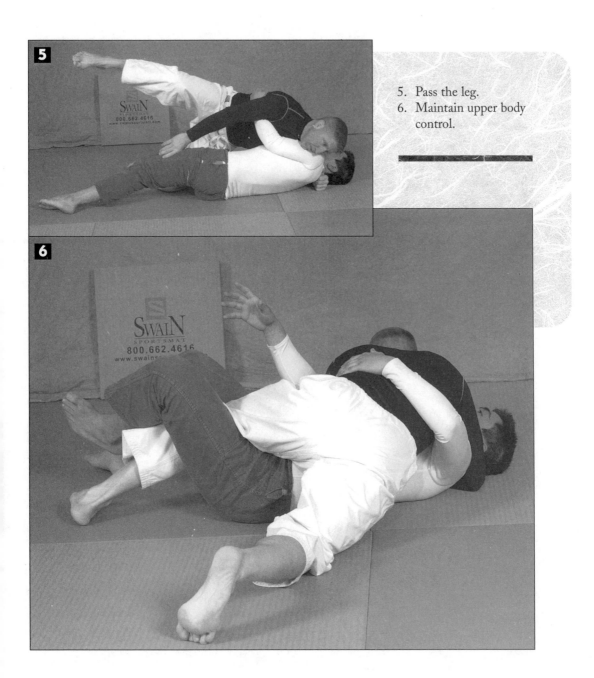

5. Pass the leg.
6. Maintain upper body control.

53

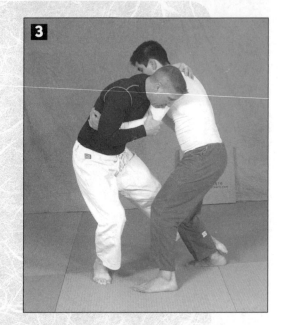

1. Starting from the under/over clinch,
2. Attack a far leg takedown, hooking behind the opponent's knee with your heel.
3. As he reacts and pulls back, hook the close foot behind the ankle with your toe or sole of the foot.

4. Pull your body closer for more power from your rear foot.
5. Push forward for the takedown.

55

1. From the clinch,
2. Snap the head forward to make the opponent off balance as you attack the leg.
3. Quickly switch to the close leg for a foot sweep.

4. Drive back and diagonally to finish the throw.
5. Maintain side body control.

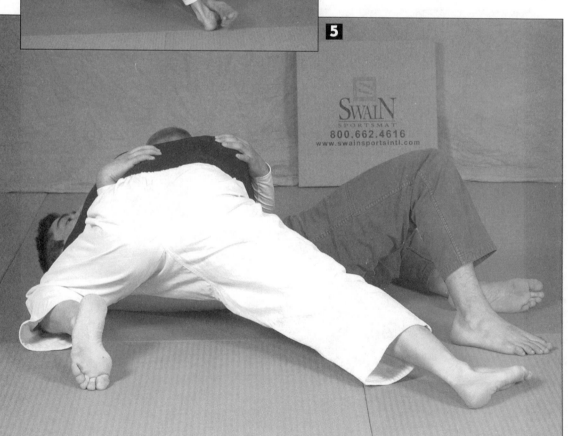

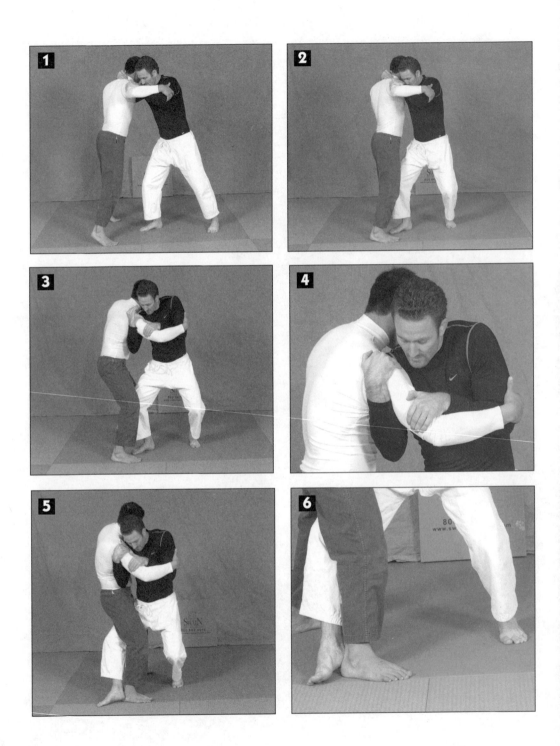

1. Start with a basic right-sided grip, right hand behind the neck controlling the head, left hand placed on the bicep.
2. Begin to step forward with right leg between the opponent's legs.
3. Release right arm from behind the neck bring it under opponent's right arm.
4. Close-up of proper grip positioning.
5. Use right leg to block /hook your opponent's right leg.
6–7. Illustrations of different ways to block the leg.
8. Drive your weight forward by pushing off with your left leg.
9. Keep your face toward your opponent. Do not give up your back.
10. Finish the technique by crossing your left leg over your right to gain top position on the ground.

1. Start with both hands on the inside, clinched behind your opponent's neck.
2. Begin movement by pulling down on the head.
3. This downward movement should create an opposite reaction from your opponent.
4. Release both hands simultaneously, bringing your hands under the armpits for a bear hug.

5. Lunge your body forward to close the distance, keep your back erect, and trap your opponent's right leg with your left.
6. Finish the throw by lifting your opponent up and toward the left, pushing off the ground with your right leg.

61

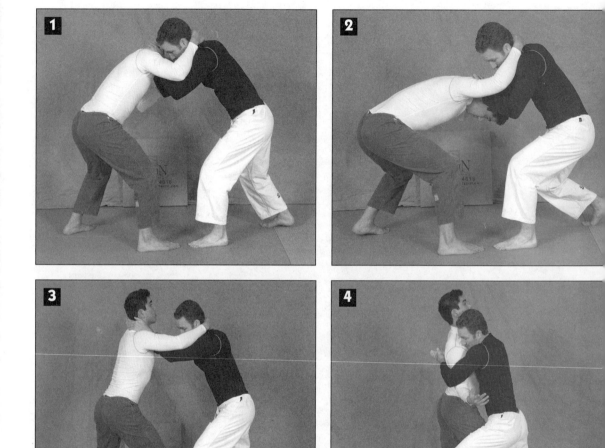

1. Start with both hands on the inside, clinched behind your opponent's neck.
2. Begin movement by pulling down on the head.
3. This downward movement should create an opposite reaction, with your opponent rising.
4. Release both hands simultaneously, bringing your right hand under the armpit, clinching hands behind the opponent's back, and trapping his right arm with your left arm.

5. Finish the throw by lifting your opponent up and toward
   the left, pushing off the ground with your right leg.

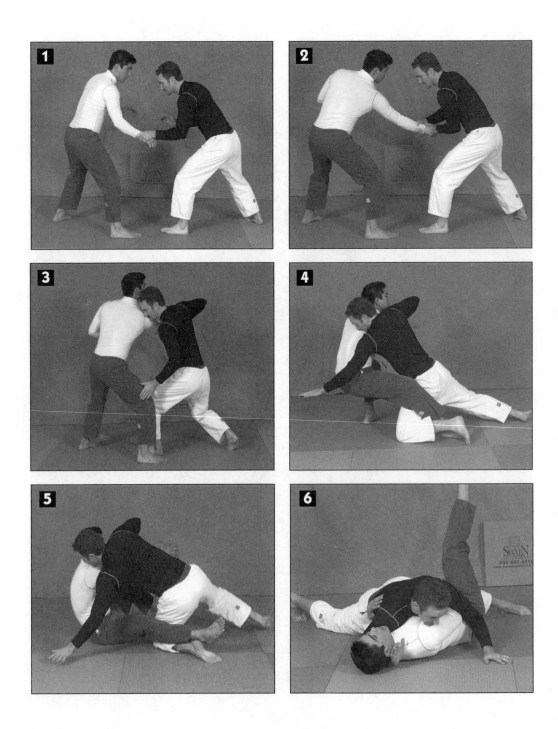

1. Start with left hand controlling opponent's right hand.
2. Bring your right hand forward to a 2-on-1 situation.
3. Do an arm-drag, pulling your opponent's right arm across with your right hand as your move forward.
4. Use an inside trip with your left leg and lunge your weight forward.
5. Lower your weight from a standing position to your knees as your opponent falls back.
6. As you hit the ground, quickly jump toward your right to get past your opponent's left leg.
7. You should end up in a side-top position, controlling the upper body.

FORWARD THROWS

The forward throws is categorized by any throw
which off-balances and throws the opponent
forward. In classical judo, forward throws are
further broken down by leg, hip, or hand,
emphasizing the main body part contributing
to the throw. In this clinch book for MMA, we
keep a more general approach to simplify the
teaching. Most forward throws are complex
motor skills, because your body must understand balance, timing, and the principle of
push-pull. When your opponent is pushing,
you must pull and vice versa. Knowing how
to set up or make your opponent move is the
key; it takes experience and much repetition.

1. From the under/over clinch,
2. Pull your arm out and take the wrist.
3. Put your forehead into the side of his face or temple area.
4. Bring your back foot close to your other foot and pull the wrist hand and arm straight out, away from your body.
5. Step across and pull opponent over your leg. Try not to step deep or toward your opponent; instead leave space so you can pull him to you.
6. Rotate body and drop your shoulder to complete the throw.
7. Go down to the ground for side control.

1. From the under hook and wrist clinch,
2. Step in front the opponent's close foot and pop his leg back while pulling toward the arm.
3. Quickly step across while he is off balance for the throw.

4. Rotate your body to finish the throw.
5. Hug the far arm just below the elbow, to apply the armlock.

1. Starting from an under hook and wrist,
2. Slide into a rear leg trip by posting your foot behind the opponent's heel.
3. As the opponent steps back to escape, pull forward with the wrist hand/arm.
4. Quickly attack while your opponent is off balance.
5. Rotate your body to finish the throw.
6. Sit into a squat while keeping you knee in his chest. Hug his elbow into you chest.
7. Lay back into the armlock for full extension, keeping your knees pinched together and body close.

1. Starting from an under hook and wrist control,
2. Pull your opponent off balance by lifting your left arm and pulling the wrist straight out, so that your opponent posts all his weight on the forward foot.
3. Step across and pull your opponent over your leg.

4. Rotate your upper body and finish the throw.
5. Keep side control once on top.

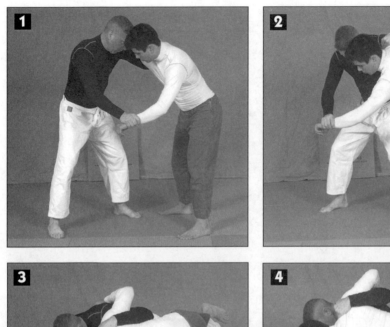

1. From an under hook and wrist control,
2. Pull your opponent forward and raise your elbow on the under hook.
3. Kick back high while pulling in a circle. It is important to understand that it is not the kicking motion of the back leg that lifts your opponent, but off-balancing and lowering your hip below his center of gravity.
4. After you extend his leg high, you step in closer to his body with your right foot.

5. Guide your opponent in a circle.
6. Maintain side control.

77

1. From under hook and wrist control,
2. Pull straight out and post your leg in front of his close leg at the same time.
3. Take a big step back with your supporting leg between his legs.

4. Rotate upper body and follow through for a big throw.

1. From under hook and wrist control,
2. Step behind opponent's heel for a backward trip.
3. As opponent steps back, pull his wrist forward to bring him onto his toes.

4. Step straight back between his legs and continue pulling in the direction of the throw.
5. Step back with your supporting foot to finish the throw.

1. From under hook and wrist control,
2. Attack an inside leg trip.
3. Maintain pulling pressure to off-balance opponent.

4. Keep his body close.
5. Rotate through to finish the throw.

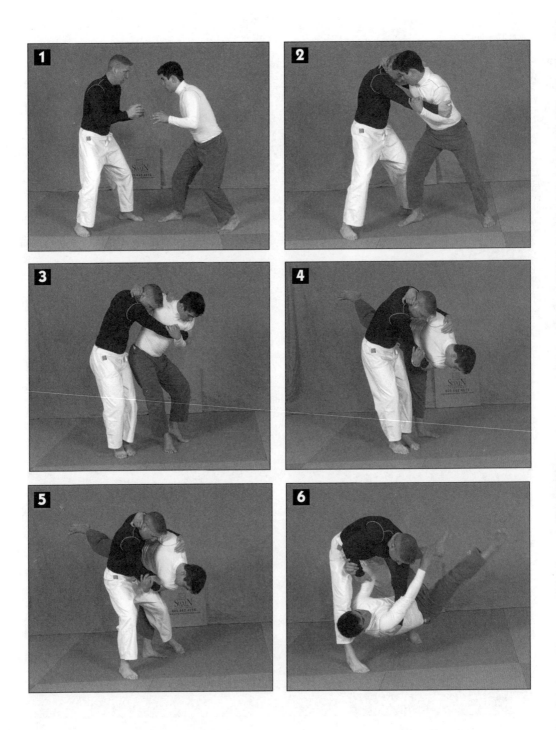

1. Starting from a free stance,
2. Opponent gets head and arm control.
3. Block with your hips first,
4. Then step out with your right foot and follow quickly with the left, so both of your feet are together.
5. Step across opponent and attack (side body).
6. Finish the throw.
7. Go down into side control.

1. Start from under hook and wrist control,
2. Step across the front foot and post.
3. As you attack, hop into your opponent in a circle.

4. Continue hopping to close into your opponent until he is thrown or falls on his own.

1. Starting from head and arm clinch,
2. Lower your core and pop the elbow up. It is important not to use too much arm strength but more body technique.
3. Lock high and bring opponent to his toes.
4. Step in for hip throw. Stomp your supporting foot on the ground as you enter, to create more explosive power.

5. Rotate your body while bringing your leg across his legs and sweeping them out.
6. Maintain side control after the throw.

1. Starting from head and arm clinch,
2. Lower your core and pop the elbow up.
3. Lock high and bring opponent to his toes.
4. Switch your stance or shuffle. The key point here is to pull down your left elbow around his neck.

5. Bend your knees and throw your hip across.
6. Spring to your toes and finish the throw.

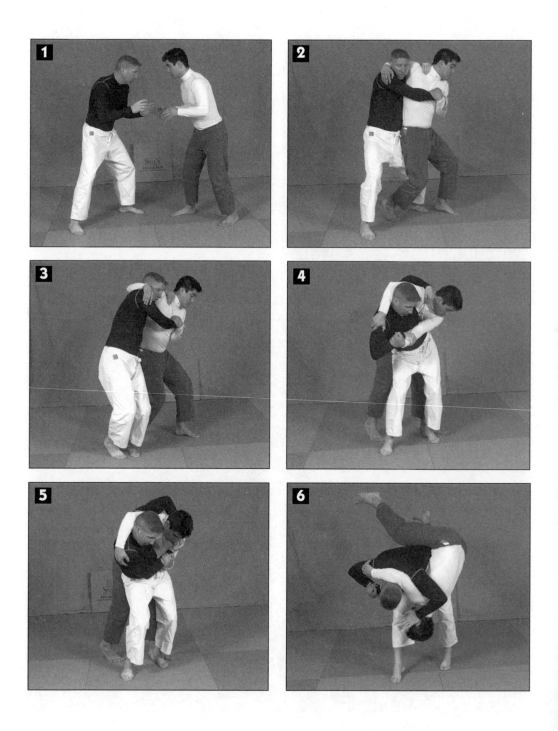

1. Starting from the open stance,
2. Lower your core and block with your hips.
3. Sidestep the lead leg.
4. Step across and hip into your opponent.
5. Pull down with your right pulling arm, and lift up with your lead shoulder.
6. Come to your toes and finish the throw.
7. Here is another angle showing the finish.

1. Starting from the open stance,
2. Gain the over hook and grab the triceps to pull them in.
3. Lower your core and stick your forehead into your opponent's temple while sliding your pulling hand down to his forearm for more control.
4. Pull in hard while stepping in with your back leg and across with your lead leg.

5. Now take a small step or hop with your supporting leg while pulling his far arm and lifting his close arm.
6. Finish the throw by rotating your body and sweeping up with your leg.

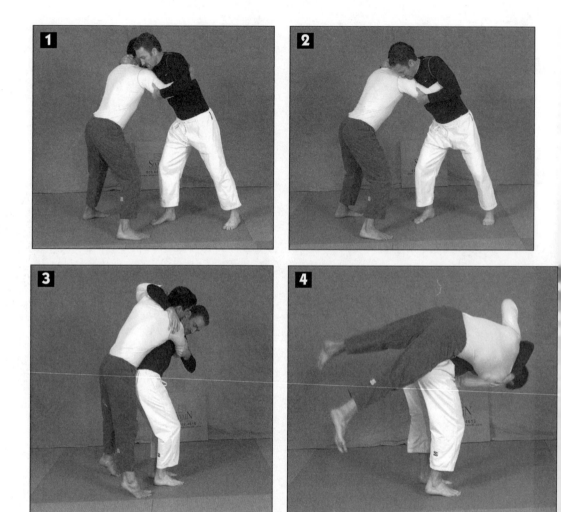

1. Start with right hand behind the neck, left hand gripping the triceps while trapping opponent's right arm under your left armpit.
2. Use your left grip to pull your opponent off balance (toward his toes).
3. Start by stepping in with your right foot, followed by your left while getting a headlock with your right arm.
4-5. Lower your hip, lift up, and turn toward your left to finish the throw.

Important points to make a hip throw work: A. Always off-balance your opponent by pulling him in. B. Always keep the upper body tight. C. Always get your center of gravity slightly below your opponent's before lifting.

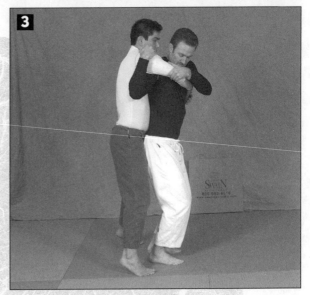

1. Start with right hand behind the neck, left hand gripping the triceps while trapping opponent's right arm under your left armpit. Pull forward to off-balance your opponent.
2. Bring your right arm under your opponent's right armpit while stepping your right leg forward.
3. Follow with your left leg turning 180 degrees to put your back against your opponent's chest; continue to pinch your opponent's arm tightly in the bend of your right elbow. Keep an upright posture.

4. Bend your knees to lower your center of gravity before you begin to spring back up.
5. Finish the throw with an explosive extension of your hips and knees while pulling your upper body down toward the left.

1. Starting point is with your right hand behind the neck. Opponent also has his right hand behind your neck. Your left hand will be in the bend of your opponent's elbow.
2. Begin technique by turning your body 180 degrees with your right leg leading your left.
3. Bring your right arm through to block your opponent's right leg from coming forward. Keep constant pressure on your left hand in the bend of the arm. A slip could result in a rear-naked choke.
4. Lower your hips to get the proper body positioning.

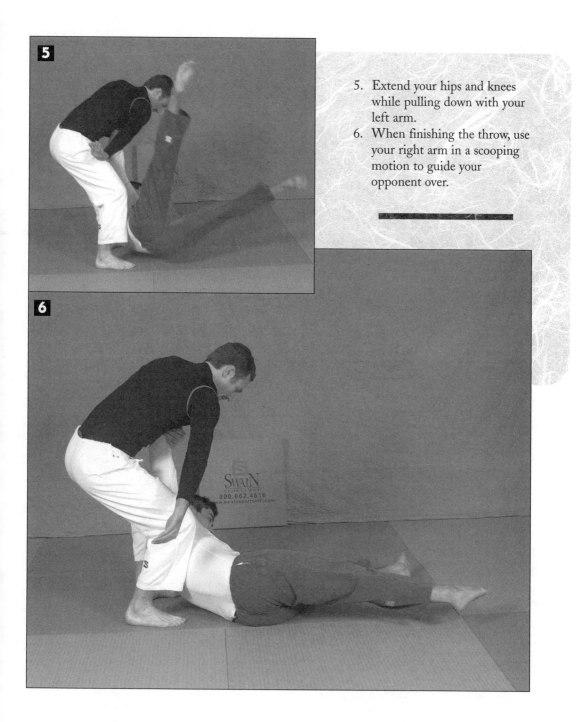

5. Extend your hips and knees while pulling down with your left arm.
6. When finishing the throw, use your right arm in a scooping motion to guide your opponent over.

1. Starting point is with your right hand behind the neck. Opponent also has his right hand behind your neck. Your left hand will be in the bend of your opponent's elbow.
2. Your opponent attempts a duck under takedown by popping your right elbow up.
3. Offensive reaction is to lower your hips and bring them back slightly, while gripping across your opponent's back to the armpit or latisimus dorsi muscle.
4. With your right leg already forward, bring your left leg around 180 degrees, pulling with your left arm.

5. This illustrates the positioning of your right hand. Use the armpit or latisimus dorsi as a handle.
6. Finish the throw with a lift of your right leg to the inner thigh of your opponent's left leg. Your left leg will need to make a very explosive extension of the knees and hip.

1. Starting position is with right arm behind the opponent's neck, left hand placed on the bicep.
2. Pull the opponent's head down to create an upward reaction. As his head comes up, move forward and place your right leg against the inside of your opponent's left thigh. Your right hand moves from around the neck to around the hip.
3. Keep your hips low as your prepare to lift; do not turn your back to your opponent.
4. Shift your weight onto your left leg (back leg) as you pull with your upper body and lift your right knee.

5. Finish the throw by lifting your right knee into your opponent's left thigh, combined with a powerful extension of your left hip and knee.

1. Staring position will have both people with the same grip: hands clinched under the arm and around the neck.
2. Both players have a right stance (right legs forward). Use your right leg to fake a leg trip.
3. This fake will make your opponent step back with his right leg.

4. Turn your body 180 degrees with your right leg leading your left.
5. Use your right leg to sweep against the inner left thigh of your opponent to make a lifting motion.

1. Starting position is same for both people: right hand behind the neck, left hand in the bend of the arm.
2. Pop up the opponent's right elbow while lunging forward with your left leg.

3. Pull down on the neck with your right arm as your left hand goes under your opponent's armpit and around to meet the opposite shoulder. Pull your opponent tight against your chest with both arms as you begin to twist your body.
4. Finish the throw by twisting your body and raising your left leg against your opponent's right inner thigh with a lifting motion.

1. Starting position is with right arm behind the opponent's neck, left hand placed on the bicep.
2. Pull the opponent's head down to create an upward reaction. As his head comes up, move forward and place your left leg against the inside of your opponent's left thigh. Your left hand moves from around his back .
3. Keep your hips low as your prepare to turn. Hold the opponent's upper body tight and close.

4. Shift your weight onto your right leg (front leg) as you pull with your upper body.
5. Finish the throw by lifting your left leg into your opponent's right thigh, combined with a powerful extension of your left hip and knee.

1. Starting with right hand behind the neck, left hand controlling the nside and gripping the bicep,

2. Turn your body 180 degrees with right leading the left. Your right hand will come under your opponent's right armpit, gripping either the upper bicep or shoulder.

3. Drop to both knees while pulling your opponent down. Two important points: Keep your left hand on the inside of the arm; otherwise you could get choked. Keep your toes extended (this way they can help push your weight forward).

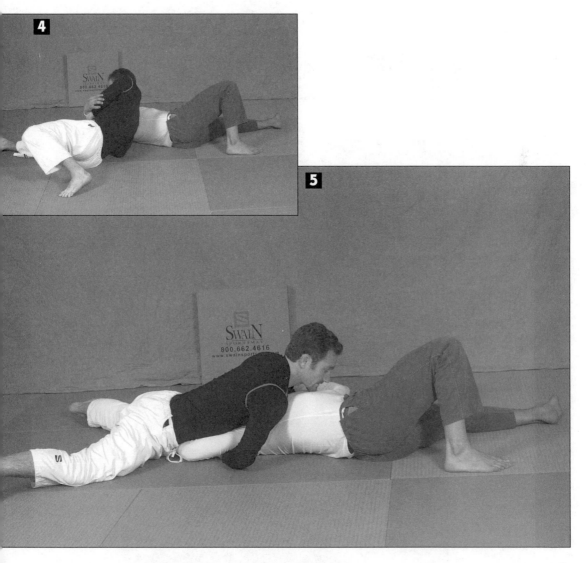

4. Twist toward your left to finish the throw.
5. Keep control of your opponent's right arm; step your left leg over your right to end in a north—south top position.

LEG SWEEPS

*Leg sweeps are a matter of off-balancing your oppo-
nent and attacking with precise timing. The most
important part of sweeps is follow-through with the
sweeping leg. The supporting leg must be slightly bent
like a spring, to push off, and the sweeping leg
straight with a sweeping motion that goes right
through the target for maximum power. There is no
hesitating with leg sweeps; it is all or nothing*

1. From a head and arm clinch,
2. Push off your back foot. The key is the snap step. Your left hand around the neck should pull your right lead foot in. This takes your opponent off balance.
3. Point the toe of the reaping leg, and try to get you hip past his hip before you bring the leg down.

4. Finish with your whole body falling forward not just your leg .
5. Maintain side control with a pin.

117

 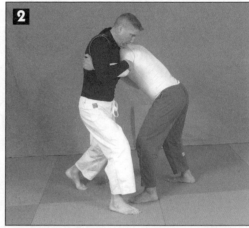

1. From a head and arm clinch,
2. In this slight variation, I show how my head arm pulls down more to make my opponent bend.
3. Now he reacts by standing up, which offers the best time to attack
4. Follow through by bring your head down.

5. Go right in for side control or pin.

1. Starting in a head and arm clinch,
2. Lower your core, stepping forward with your back foot, which moves your opponent back.
3. As he pushes back, pivot your back leg and catch his lead leg just at the ankle with the sole of your foot.

4. Sweep through with your leg.
5. Use your upper body to guide your opponent down.

1. From a double over hook clinch,
2. Lower your core and step forward, pushing your opponent back.
3. As he pushes back, pivot your back leg and catch his lead leg just at the ankle with the sole of your foot.

4. Sweep through with your leg.
5. Fall right into hold-down, with hooks if possible.

1. Starting from the under hook and wrist,
2. Step into opponent with back foot while pushing the wrist back.
3. As he pushes back, pull the wrist hand hard, straight out.
4. Sweep with your leg as straight as possible. The supporting leg should be bent, and do not forget to pivot on the ball of your foot.

5. Maintain side control with key lock.

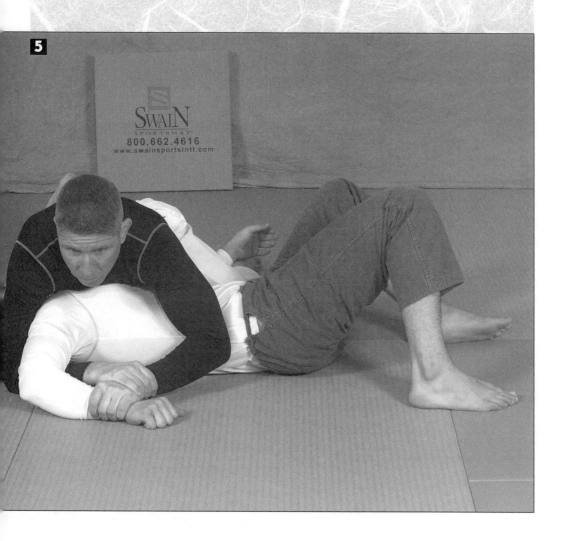

1. Opponent locks your body from the front.
2. Lower your core to stop his momentum while taking the two over hooks.
3. As he stands, push forward turn and sweep.

4. Sweep through with your leg.
5. Pull the head up for maximum control.

1. From the head and arm clinch,
2. Drop your hand and body so the opponent feels all your weight.
3. Keeping your head down and weight posted, shoot your leg and arm across, trapping his leg.
4. Lower your head and body for the throw to his side.

5. Maintain side control after the throw.

1. From head and arm clinch,
2. Block the strike with your elbow.
3. As the knee comes down, turn the opposite way for the sweep, using opponent's own momentum. This is felt, and not something you can hesitate executing.

4. The finish of this sweep is performed more with your body. Do not try to lift your sweeping leg high, but maintain balance with both feet.

1. Opponent gains control of under hook and wrist.
2. He starts to set up for an attack.
3. As you feel him push forward, turn and slide your arm down and step across to trap the ankle.
4. Finish with shoulder in the side. This is a hard fall so be careful.

5. Pop back up and sit into a cross armlock.

1. Starting from the clinch,
2. Step in a circle and pull down on his neck,
3. Continue in a circle until his feet come together,
4. Sweep the legs out as one foot comes into the other.

5. Extend the leg out as far as possible.
6. Use your arm across his neck to redirect him down. This sweep is pure timing, and will take much practice to perfect.

1. From the clinch, attack the far leg with an outer reap throw, to make the opponent step back
2. Reverse step and hook the close leg while coming hard into a high clinch.
3. Lifting with your knee, hoist your opponent off the ground.

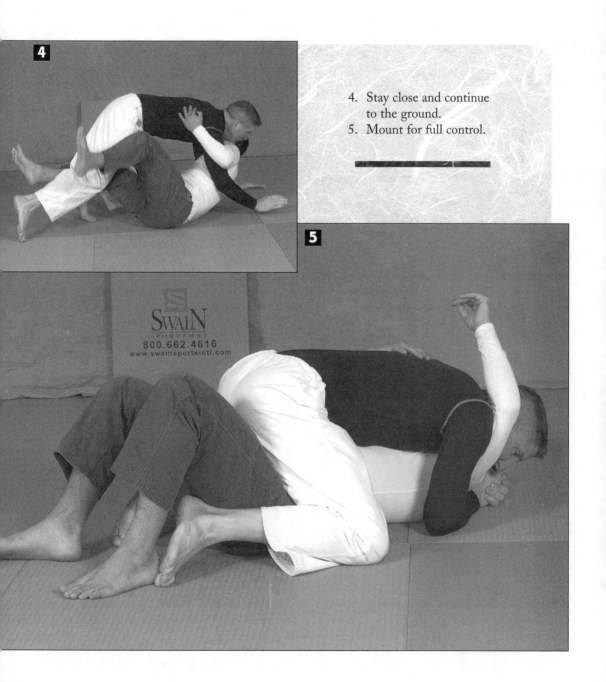

4. Stay close and continue to the ground.
5. Mount for full control.

137

LEG PICK TAKEDOWNS

This category emphasizes grabbing one or both legs to take your opponent down. It is important to understand that these are not throws, but takedowns, and the focus is not on picking up your opponent for the crowd pleaser slam, but quickly catching him off balance and putting him down into a positive ground position for a submission.

1. Starting from the clinch,
2. Lower your core and step in, dropping your right shoulder and posting his foot with your foot.
3. Grab behind the calf and let your hand slide up to behind the knee as you push forward.
4. Drive forward with your shoulder to apply pressure while pushing the knee down to pass.

5. Pass the leg and put your knee to the ground.
6. Control the head and arm for the pin or choke.

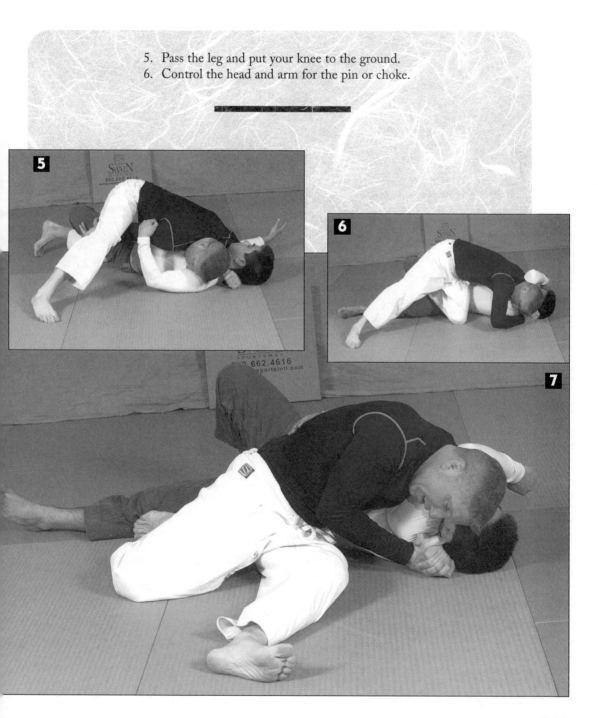

1. From the clinch,
2. Shoot your neck hand high so your bicep hits your opponent's throat and your other hand grabs the back of the knee.
3. Drive forward to pass his legs.
4. Control the upper body.

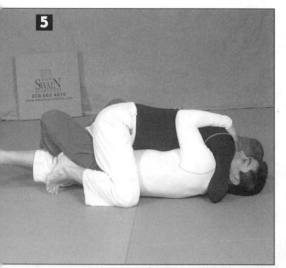

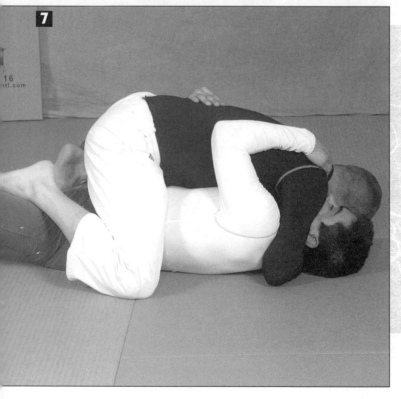

5. Change the upper grip to better control his head.
6. Walk your foot up close to his body and escape to mount.
7. Control the head and arm for the pin or choke.

1. Starting from the clinch,
2. Lower your core and step in, dropping your right shoulder and trying to sweep the opponent's left leg.
   The opponent reacts by moving his leg back.
3. Bring you leg back to the original position.

4. And drive forward with your left leg as you grab the opponent's right inner thigh to apply pressure while pulling the leg up.
5. Then, you bring him to the ground and apply a side control.

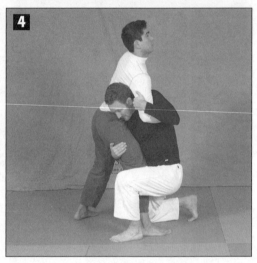

1. Starting with right hand behind the neck, left hand controlling the inside, gripping the bicep,
2. Pull down on the neck.
3. Opponent reacts with upward movement.
4. Step left leg forward on the outside, with right leg on the knee on the inside. Head ducks under the armpit with your left arm, pulling opponent's right arm tight against the back of your neck.

5. Finish the technique by pushing your opponent forward and slightly to the left, while rolling your upper body toward the left side.

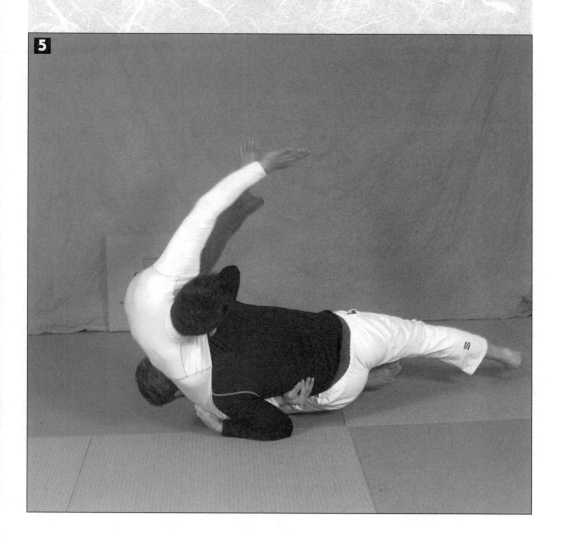

1. Start with right hand behind the neck, left hand controlling the inside and gripping the biceps.
2. Pull down on the neck.
3. Opponent reacts with upward movement.
4. Move your left arm to trap opponent's right arm as you lunge forward with your left leg. Your forehead will hit directly in the chest of your opponent, as you pull his body down with his right arm that is trapped under your left armpit.
5. Finish the throw by picking the right leg of your opponent and driving forward with as much force as possible. It is important to keep your back erect to generate force and close the distance between your and our opponent.

PICK UPS

The focus here is on using your whole body, especially your hips, to lift your opponent off his feet and return him to the ground on his back. This usually occurs as a counter to a throw where you block first with your hips to stop his inertia, then reverse the momentum, using his power and energy to throw him.

1. Starting from the clinch,
2. Duck under opponent's arm
3. Keep your head close to his side.

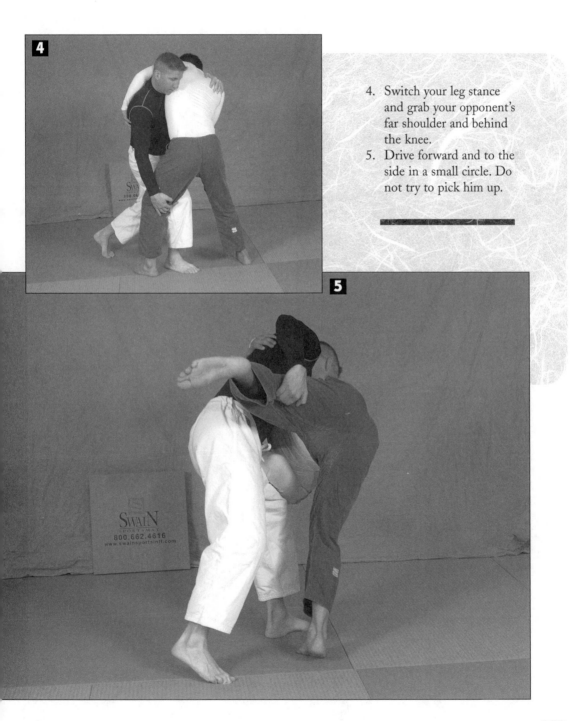

4. Switch your leg stance and grab your opponent's far shoulder and behind the knee.
5. Drive forward and to the side in a small circle. Do not try to pick him up.

153

1. A back view shown after the leg switch.
2. This time, step straight into opponent, catching his shin with your foot turned in.

3. Lift straight up with your hip and rotate to finish the throw.

1. Starting from the under hook and wrist,
2. Duck under opponent's arm and step deep. Remember to lower your core.
3. Use your hips, not your back, to pick up opponent.
4. Rotate body to throw.
5. Fall into side control.

 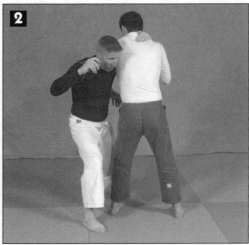

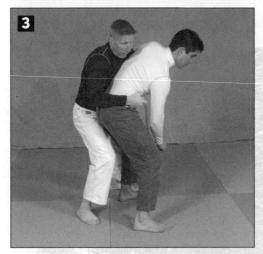 

1. From the free stance,
2. Duck under opponent.
3. Gain back control, locking your hands.
4. Drop your core and back hand to reach his inside thigh.

5. Lift with your hips.
6. Rotate like a clock to finish the throw.

1. Starting with right hand behind the neck, left hand controlling the inside, gripping the bicep,
2. Pull down on the neck.
3. Opponent reacts with upward movement.

4. Duck your head under your opponent's right armpit, pulling his arm tight against the neck with your left arm. Be sure to have his right arm trapped under your left armpit. Your right leg (inside leg) will remain on your foot with your knee up; your left knee will be on the ground. Extend your back and pull down with your left arm to lift and finish the throw.

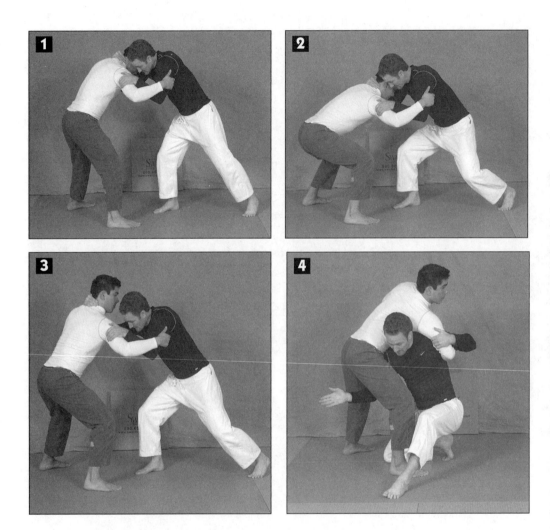

1. Starting with right hand behind the neck, left hand controlling the inside, gripping the bicep,
2. Pull down on the neck.
3. Opponent reacts with upward movement.
4. Duck your head under your opponent's right armpit, pulling his arm tight against the neck with your left arm. Be sure to have his right arm trapped under your left armpit. Your left leg will lead forward; it will be placed on the outside of your opponent's right leg as your reach through with your right arm.

5. Opponent sprawls back to defend the lift.
6. This illustrates the proper positioning for hand on the elbow held tightly against the neck. It is important not to leave any space.
7. When the opponent sprawls his feet back to defend the lift, he is now off balance to the front. Simply sit your left leg out (similar to a hurdler's position), roll back toward your left shoulder (do not go flat to your back).

1. Starting with right hand behind the neck, left hand controlling the inside, gripping the bicep,
2. This is a different approach, as this time we will attack the opposite side. Duck under your opponent's right arm (stepping forward with your left leg) as you simultaneously slide your right arm from the neck down to the triceps.
3. This time your left leg is on his foot while your right leg is on the knee.

4. As you begin to lift, your opponent sprawls. If he does not sprawl, you can lift and finish the throw.
5. To finish the throw, lunge forward, putting your weight on your left leg so you can sit your right leg out to the hurdler's position. Sit back toward your right shoulder at a slight angle; do not fall flat on your back.

1. Starting position is the same for both fighters: Right hand behind the neck, left arm on the triceps or in the bend of the opponent's elbow.
2. Pull down on the neck to create an upward reaction, pop the elbow up as your come forward with your left leg. Keep your back in an erect position.
3. Simultaneously lower your right arm from the neck to your opponent's left triceps. Bring your left hand through the middle of the legs to prepare for the lift.

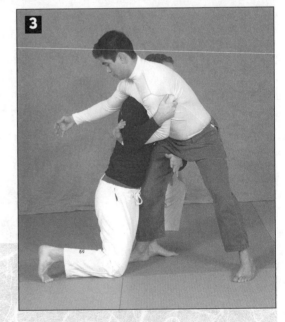

4. Lunge forward to a standing position, lifting your opponent off the floor. Keep an erect posture to ensure an easy and safe lift. Keep good control of the triceps with your right hand.

5. Finish the throw with a scooping motion, pulling down with your right and lifting with your left hand.

1. Starting position is the same for both fighters. Right hand should be placed behind the neck, left arm on the triceps or in the bend of the opponent's elbow.
2. Pull down on the neck to create an upward reaction, pop the elbow up as you come forward with your left leg. Keep your back in an erect position.
3. Simultaneously lower your right arm from the neck to your opponent's left triceps. Bring your left hand through the middle of the legs to prepare for the lift.

4. As you begin to lift, you will change the direction by releasing the triceps and going back toward the neck with your right hand (cross face motion).
5. Finish the throw with an explosive extension of the knees and hips. At the end of your extension, cross face with your right hand while simultaneously sweeping the leg with your left leg.

1. Starting position is the same for both fighters. Right hand should be placed behind the neck, left arm on the triceps or in the bend of the opponents elbow.
2. Pull down on the neck to create an upward reaction, pop the elbow up as your come forward with your left leg. Keep your back in an erect position.
3. Bring your left hand through the middle of the legs to prepare for the lift
4. Bring your right hand from the neck down to the triceps.
5. Pull your right arm down toward the floor as you move in circular motion.
6. Finish the throw by raising your left leg and pulling in a circular motion with your right arm. It is not necessary to lift your opponent off the ground to make this throw work. Simply twist him to the floor.
7. This illustration shows proper positioning for this technique. This is a technique that is often used as a counter when people attempt an inside leg throw.

1. Starting position is the same for both fighters. Right hand should be placed behind the neck, left arm on the triceps or in the bend of the opponents elbow.
2. Pull down on the neck to create an upward reaction; pop the elbow up as your come forward with your left leg.
3. Your opponent tries to counter your lift with an outside leg trip. When the leg trip is attempted, be sure not to continue with a forward momentum. You should now take advantage of your opponent's weakness to his backside.

4. Rather than moving your right hand down to the triceps, as in similar situations, this time you will keep your hand up around the neck as you lift with a sweeping motion toward the back to finish the technique.

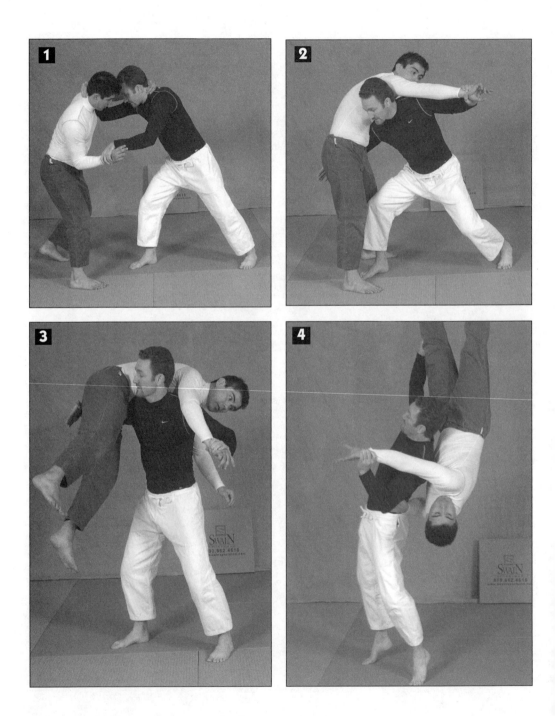

1. Starting with your right hand on the neck of your opponent, left hand controlling your opponent's right wrist,
2. Release the neck with your right hand as you duck under and lunge forward with your right foot. You should aim your right shoulder to the lower abdomen or hip of your opponent.
3. Remember to keep good posture with an upright stance as you close the distance to your opponent.
4. This throw requires not only explosive power, but perfect timing. The angle to finish this technique is directly over your shoulder to the back.
5. In competition, rather than letting your opponent fly, you should come down on top to secure an offensive position on the ground. Always keep a hold with your left hand.

REAR TAKEDOWNS

We define any move that takes the opponent directly to his back as a rear takedown. In order to make these techniques effective, it is better to make your opponent pull back from a clinch, so you can follow his power and momentum. Attacking with a forward throw and combining it with a rear takedown is the key.

1. From the clinch.
2. Duck under step in.
3. High clinch drive his shoulder up.
4. As the opponent pulls his shoulder down, step in and hook his leg, heel to heel.

5. Drive straight back, keeping his shoulders up.
6. Fall into a side mount or choke.

179

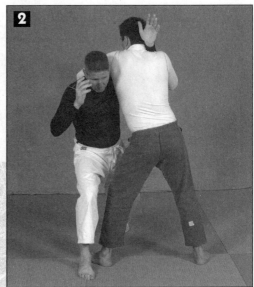

1. Here is another view from the back, starting from the clinch.
2. Duck under and drive your arm straight and up.
3. Take his body straight back.

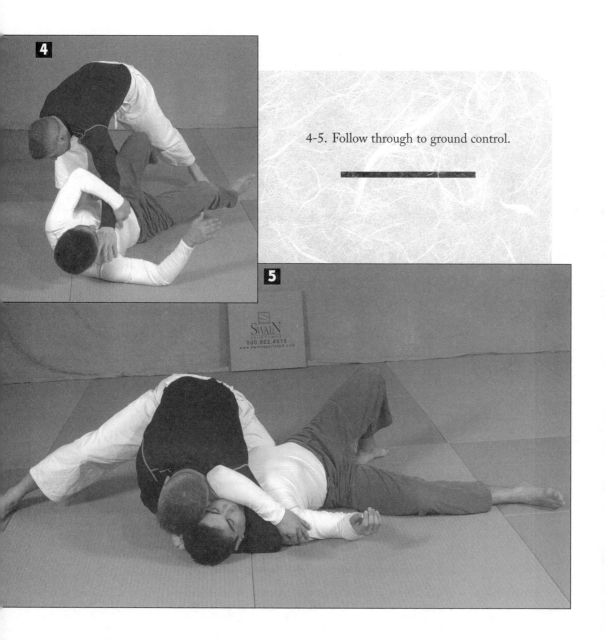

4-5. Follow through to ground control.

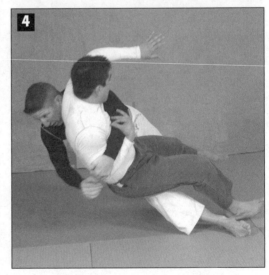

1. From the free stance,
2-3. Duck under to back control.
4. Lower core and slide leg behind both of opponent's legs.

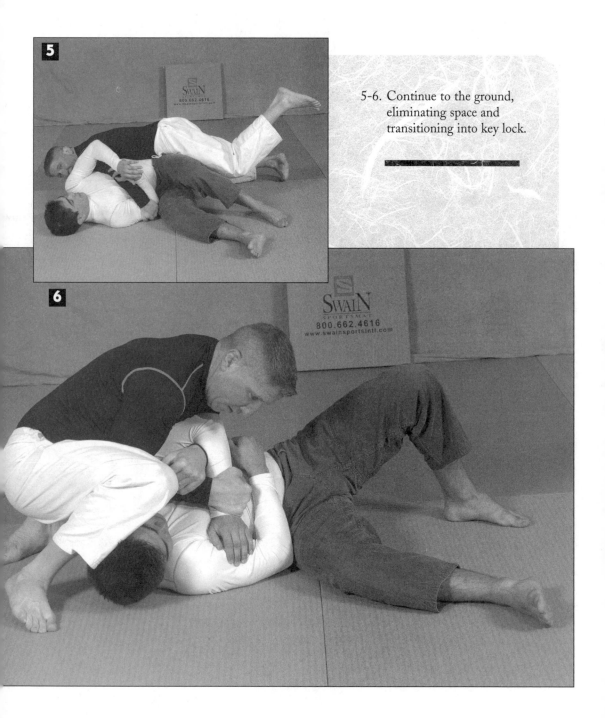

5-6. Continue to the ground, eliminating space and transitioning into key lock.

1. Starting in free stance,
2. Duck under your opponent.
3. Gain back control.
4. Step inside far leg.

5. Sit back, hugging opponent, and bring him straight back.
6. Move to side control.

1. Starting from head and arm,
2. Block the throw with your hips.
3. Gain back control.

4-5. As opponent stands back up to escape, hoist to the rear with hips.

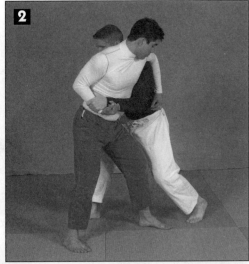

1. Starting in free stance,
2. Duck under and control opponent's far arm.
3. Move to opponent's other side and control his arm by trapping it to his side.

4. Keep body lock tight while falling to the side.

1. Starting position here requires a little bit of distance. Gain control of your opponent's right hand with your left hand.
2. Using an arm drag, cross grip with your right hand and pull your opponent toward you.
3. As your opponent comes toward you, your left hand will go over his arm and scoop toward his leg.
4. Continue to pull tight with you right arm as your sit all your weight on your opponent's arm. At the same time, you should be grabbing your opponent's right leg.
5. Finish the takedown by falling backward, maintaining a tight clinch on your opponent's arm.
6. Once on the ground, you must use the momentum of the fall to continue toward your opponent.
7. One option is an arm lock. This will work as long as you maintain good control of your opponent's wrist throughout the technique.
8. Throw your right leg over your opponent to gain the top position.
9. Once on top, there are numerous techniques to choose from, as you are in a very good offensive position. Never relax once you complete a good throw; your opponent's instincts will be very quick to bounce up to avoid being beaten.

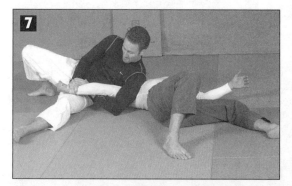

1. Starting with a cross grip, right hand controlling your opponent's right hand,
2. Move to a 2-on-1 grip, with your left hand placed above your right hand on the wrist. Be sure to have your four fingers on the inside to allow proper movement for the next step.
3. Step in close with your left leg placed slightly outside your opponent's right foot. Place your right elbow on the inside of your opponent's arm.
4. You can now release your right grip as your step forward with your right leg. Place your right hand on the inside thigh of your opponent.

5. Complete the throw by putting your weight on your opponent's arm with an explosive lift, arching your back toward your left shoulder as you lift the leg with your right hand.

6. Proper positioning allows for no space between you and your opponent. The smallest amount of space will cause your opponent to land flat on top of you.

1. Starting with a cross grip, right hand controlling your opponent's right hand,
2. Move to a 2-on-1 grip, with your left hand placed above your right hand on the wrist. Be sure to have your four fingers on the inside to allow proper movement for the next step.
3. Step in close with your left leg placed slightly outside your opponent's right foot. Place your right elbow on the inside of your opponent's arm.

4. Take a short step toward your opponent, placing your right arm on the outside of his right knee. Put your weight on your opponent's arm with force toward the side.
5. Finish the technique by falling to your back left side, taking your opponent almost directly to his right side.

195

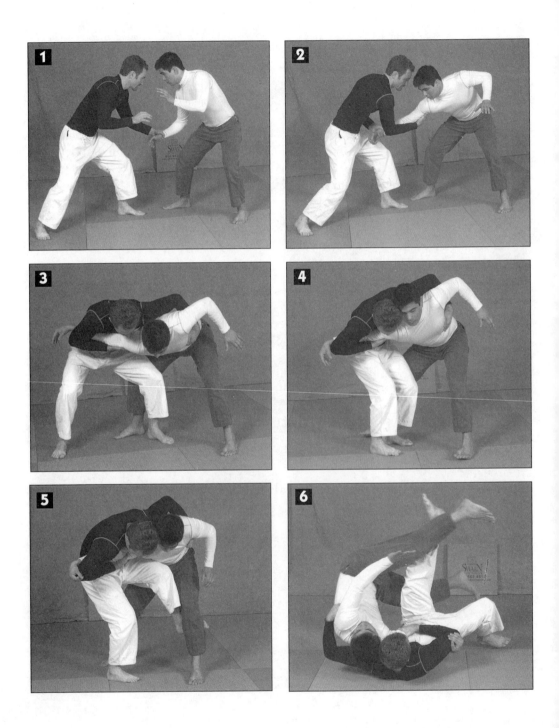

1. The starting position requires a little bit of distance between the players. Control your opponent's right hand with your left hand.
2. Cross grip by pulling your opponent toward your right side, taking a grip with your right hand on the inside of the triceps.
3. Pull your opponent's right arm across your chest, putting your weight on the shoulder to keep him from standing up straight. Your left arm will go across the back, gripping onto the armpit or latisimus dorsi muscle. Left leg should be placed just inside your opponent's right leg.
4. Step your right leg inside, next to your left leg, as you begin to pull your opponent forward.
5. Bring your left leg up into the bend of the knee or inside thigh of your opponent
6. Squat down to make a ball, then spring back, pushing off the floor with your right leg.
7. Finish the move by completing a backward roll, ending with top control.

1. Start from no particular grip for either player.
2. Move forward with your left hand over the top of your opponent's arm and under the armpit.
3. Raise your left leg over the knee of your opponent's left leg, closer to the hip if possible.
4. Usually the opponent will react by grabbing your leg. This is not a problem.

5. Hop to a position that is parallel to your opponent's.
6. Jump into the air, crossing your right leg behind the bend of the knee, making a scissor motion to collapse your opponent. You can use your arm to support the weigh of your body, if necessary.
7. Illustration shows the finish of the throw.

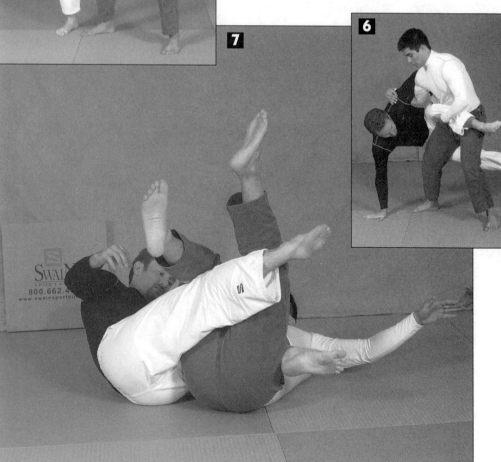

199

1. Starting from a free stance,
2. Opponent takes an offensive step by getting an over grip with his right hand.
3. Place your left hand around the back of your opponent's waist, gripping tightly. Your right hand will take a grip on your opponent's right ankle with your four fingers on the inside.
4. Step your left leg behind your opponent's left leg

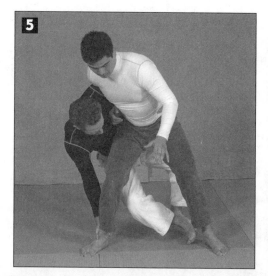

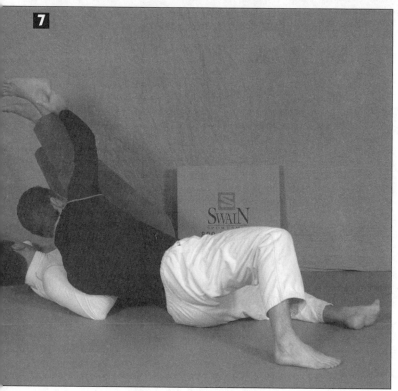

5. Begin to slide your right leg toward the middle of your opponent's legs as you fall toward the side.
6. Pull back with your left hand on the hip, and push up on the ankle with your right hand.
7. Finish the move by pushing the ankle as high into the air as possible while you come up to gain a top ground position.

ARMLOCK TAKEDOWNS

These are very sophisticated grappling moves, which have a low percentage of working in a major competition. However, they send a clear message of who is in charge when you are in a clinch. The pain of getting halfway caught causes hesitation by your opponent. The key for these moves is anticipation and small body movement in order not to telegraph.

1. Starting in free stance, control opponent's wrist as he reaches forward for your neck.
2. Quickly pull forward across your chest.

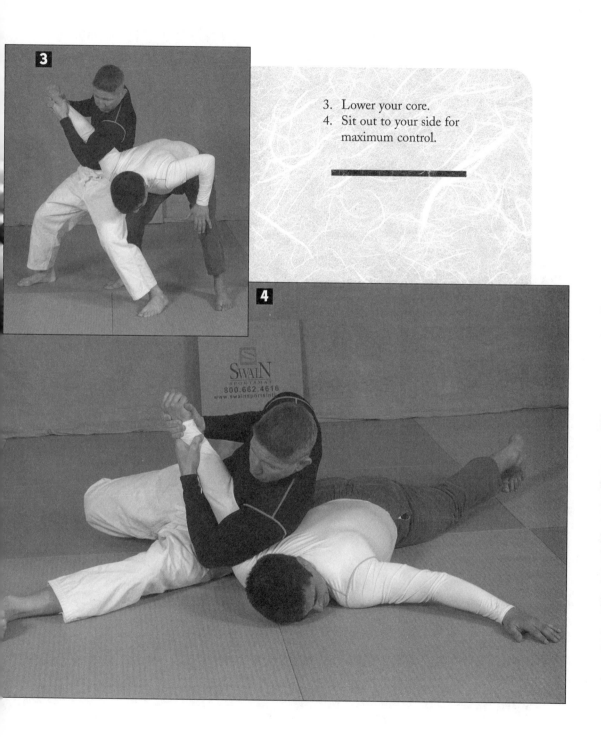

3. Lower your core.
4. Sit out to your side for maximum control.

INTRO—Standing armlocks take precise timing and technique to work. Your opponent must make a mistake by reaching too far or hesitating in a vulnerable position.

1. Starting in free stance,
2. Gain the under hook.
3. Control the shoulder as much as possible.
4. Turn your chest and his pull arm in.
5. Close up of proper hand placement.

6. Bend the front knee
7. Then cup your hands around opponent's elbow joint.
8-9. Take a large step back in a circular motion until opponent falls to the ground.
10-11. Spin to the other side and sit for the cross-body armlock.

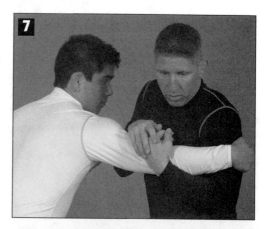

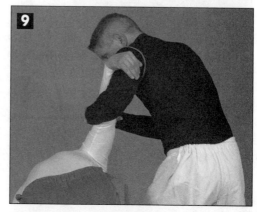

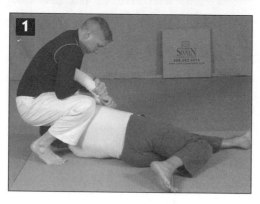

1. Starting with a controlling grip on your opponents left hand,
2. Cross grip with your left hand to the left arm of your opponent, gripping tightly on the triceps.
3. Pull your opponent across, putting all of your weight on him until he falls to his knees.
4. As he falls, use your right leg to hook his left arm. Keep your weight on him to make sure he doesn't try to stand up.

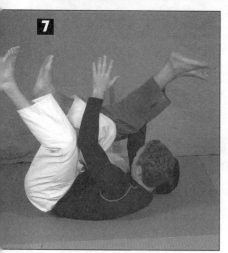

5. Your right arm will move toward your opponent's shoulder. R reach down toward your opponent's left knee as you position yourself for a roll.
6. You will begin to make a right side shoulder roll, taking your opponent's arm with you.
7. As you roll through, keep control of your opponent's arm with your right leg, holding onto his leg with your right arm.
8. Finish the arm lock by sitting up and pulling your hips back

DEFENSES

A strong defense is a constant offense; however no one can go all out for the entire match, so having a good defense against basic moves is a necessity. These are some basic and advanced defenses against your high percentage attacks, like double legs and basic throws. The proper stance in blocking throws or takedowns with your hips, and not just your upper body strength, is the key.

1. Starting with distance between the players,
2. Opponent shoots in for a single leg takedown. Defend by pulling your right leg back and lowering your hips
3. Take a grip with your left hand over the top of your opponent's right arm, then through the armpit. As he lifts the leg, be sure to keep your leg in the middle of the opponent's legs. This way, he can't lift them too high.
4. Take a grip with your right hand on top of your opponent's right hand that is holding your leg.

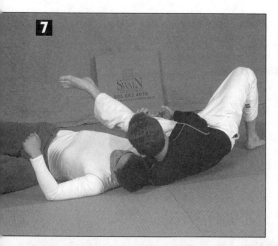

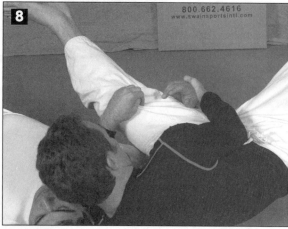

5. Hop your right leg closer to the inside as your sit your weight on your opponent's hand. Make a ball as a squat down and push off with your right leg.
6. Use your leg as a guide to kick him over. It should be place in the bend of your opponent's knee.
7. Landing position.
8. Close up of the grip on the hand. During the roll, you should be pulling the hand very tight.
9. Finish the move by rolling all the way backward to a top position.

1. Starting with distance between the players,
2. Opponent shoots in for a single leg takedown. Defend by pulling your right leg back and lowering your hips.
3. With your left hand, grab your opponent's left wrist.

4. Begin to pull your right hand as your turn your body 180 degrees and lift your left leg to the inner thigh of your opponent.
5. Continue to pull with your left hand as your twist your body toward the right side.
6. Finish the throw, coming down directly onto your opponent.

215

1. Starting with distance between the players,
2. Opponent shoots in for a single leg takedown. Defend by pulling your right leg back and lowering your hips.
3. Take a grip with your left hand over the top of your opponent's right arm, then through the armpit. As he lifts his leg, be sure to keep your leg in the middle of the opponent's legs. This way, he can't lift too high.
4. Extend your left leg to place it in the bend of your opponent's left knee.
5. Hop your right leg around the side, placing it near your opponent's right foot. Reach with your right arm down to the bend of your opponent's right knee.
6. Finish the move by rolling backward, collapsing your opponent's knees.
7. Once on the ground, quickly throw your right leg over your left to take the top ground position.

1. Starting with distance between the players,
2. Opponent shoots in for a single leg takedown. Defend by pulling your right leg back and lowering your hips.
3. Take a grip with your left hand over the top of your opponent's right arm, then through the armpit. As he lifts his leg, be sure to keep your leg in the middle of the opponent's legs. This way, he can't lift them too high.
4. Extend your left leg to place it in the bend of your opponent's left knee.

5. Step forward with your right leg, squat down and push off the ground while cross- facing your opponent. Use your left leg to kick him over, placing your leg in the bend of his left knee.

6. When done properly, this move should end with you in a perfect top position.

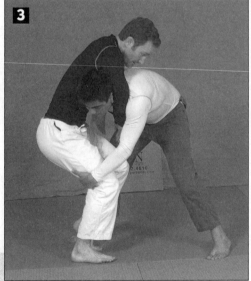

1. Starting with some distance between the players,
2. Opponent attempts a double leg takedown. Sprawl back with your right leg, letting the opponent have your left leg. Shoot your left arm through the armpit and your right arm under the neck. This should secure a very tight head lock.
3. Begin to rise, bringing your opponent's head up. In the process, your right leg will come forward as he will try to capture both legs for the takedown.

4. Bring your left leg up to the bend of your opponent's left leg as you begin to roll back.
5. This move should end with you on top, locked into a very tight choke with your right arm.

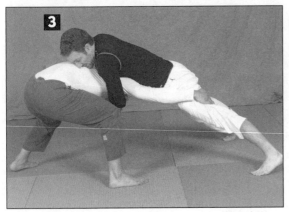

1. Starting with some distance between the players,
2. Opponent attempts a single leg take down. Sprawl back and lower your hips to avoid the takedown.
3. Since the opponent has one leg locked up, you should sprawl back with both legs to make him loosen the grip on your left leg.
4. As your opponent begins to release your leg, using your left hand, push his right arm across his body.
5. Capture his right arm with your right hand.
6. Do a cross leg pick with your left hand on your opponent's left leg.

7. Finish the move by driving forward. The opponent should be unable to step back as you have his leg trapped.
8. This move should put you directly on top with solid control of the upper body.

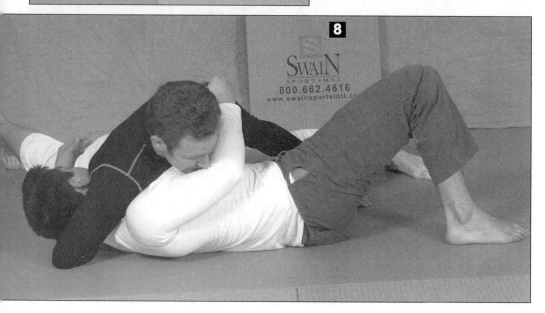

1. Starting with some distance between the players,
2. Opponent shoots a single leg takedown with his head on the inside.
3. With your right arm, push his head down so he collapses onto his knees.
4. Tuck your right heel into the bend of your opponent's left armpit.
5. Reach to your opponent's right arm with both hands. Grasp a good hold of his arm to prepare the roll.
6. As you roll toward the side, you will secure a figure-four lock on your opponent's head and left arm.
7. Pull the arm across the face to tighten your figure-four leg lock.
8. One option is to finish the move with an armlock by push the trapped arm forward.

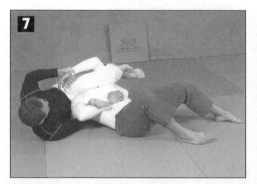 

9. The other option is to finish with a choke. Grab the inside of the near leg to pull yourself forward. Turning your hips this direction should tighten the choke enough for submission.

1. One person starting with and over grip and one with an under grip,
2. Opponent attempts an inside leg pick.
3. You allow the opponent to lift your leg as you place it between his legs.
4. Keeping your over hook with your right arm, wrap your right leg around the inside of your opponent's left leg. Hook your toe on the outside from extra grip.

5. Get control of your opponent's right arm with your left hand.
6. Kick your right leg forward as your sit and fall toward the back.

1. Starting with distance between the players,
2. Opponent shoots in for a single leg takedown. Defend by pulling your right leg back and lowering your hips.
3. Take a grip with your left hand over the top of your opponent's right arm, then through the armpit. As he lifts his leg, be sure to keep your leg in the middle of the opponent's legs. This way, he can't lift them too high.
4. Extend your left leg to place it in the bend of your opponent's left knee. Reach back to the bend of your opponent's right knee with your right hand.

5. As your opponent drives forward, you go with the momentum and roll forward in the direction of a right side shoulder roll.
6. To complete the throw, roll through, kicking your left leg up to push the opponent over completely.

1. Opponent attacks single leg.
2. Push his head to the outside.
3. Key lock the near arm.
4. Sit down and roll straight back.

5. Use his pushing momentum to roll through.
6. Control opponent with key lock.

1. Starting in free stance,
2-3. Opponent attacks a high low leg pick.
4. Counter by pivoting into a rear leg sweep.
   The key here is to control your opponent's near shoulder.

5. Rotate your body to finish throw.
6. Maintain side control.

PARTNER TRAINING

Functional training, which develops your motor skills in sport-specific exercises, is the most popular modern way to train today. Training the Core of your Body, which is your upper legs to lower torso, including your hips, stomach, and lower back is key in all combative sports. Here are some simple exercises that train your body for the Clinch and takedowns from the clinch, using only another partner.

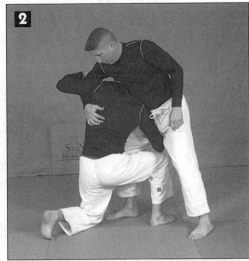

This exercise involves one person lifting his partner over his shoulders, like a fireman's carry. Once the partner is secured on the shoulders, begin to lunge forward with your left leg (picture 4). Make a 90-degree angle with your forward leg, then raise straight up. Do not bend your

forward knee past your toes. Keep a straight back with your eyes always looking forward. Always do a few repetitions without your partner for a warm-up.

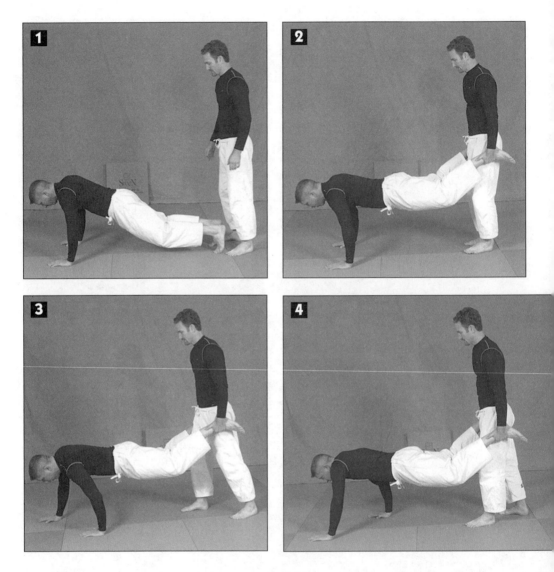

Wheel Barrel walks or push-ups are quite common in grappling. This exercise can be done several different ways. At the beginner level, it only involves walking on your hands. Once you get comfortable walking on your hands, then you can do a push-up each time your take a step. At the advanced level, you can do an explosive push-up: lunge both hands forward at the same

time to make your way down the mat. Performed at this level, the exercise becomes a great plyometric workout that develops not only upper body strength but a strong core as well.

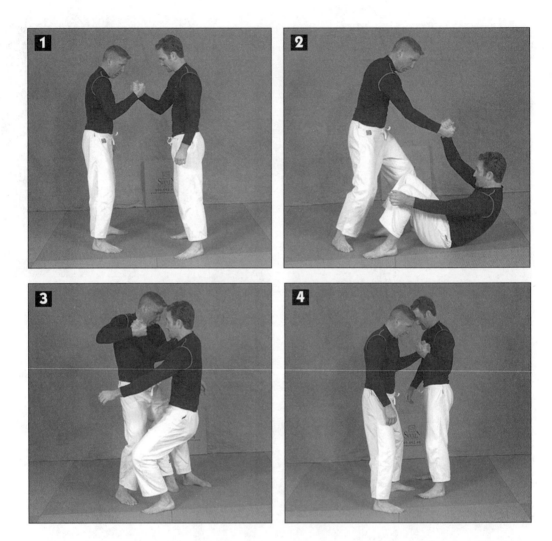

This exercise is a great workout for both partners. Start with both partners grasping each other's hands (thumbs up). One partner squats down all the way to a sitting position, then all the way down until his back is flat on the ground. Partners will work together to bring the bottom person back to the standing position. In the beginning, the standing partner can take a small step with his outside leg to help maintain balance. Once the partners are in sync and have enough strength, the top person

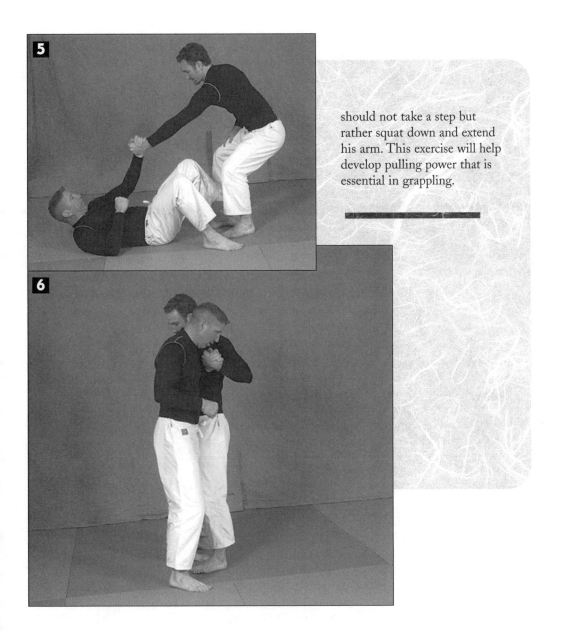

should not take a step but rather squat down and extend his arm. This exercise will help develop pulling power that is essential in grappling.

This is known as a partner clean. Similar to an Olympic lift with a barbell, one partner lifts the other, using a grip on the inside of the thigh and around the neck. The partner being lifted must keep his body rigid like a bar, with one arm thrown over the shoulder. In the starting position, the partners are chest to belly. The first movement is a slight downward motion (flexion of the

knees and hips). Keeping an upright posture, the second movement will be an explosive extension of the knees and hips. At the highest point, the partner being lifted should be facing down as his right hand swings out (picture 4).

This exercise is known as a partner dead lift. Start with one partner on all fours. The other partner will clinch his hands tightly around the chest, standing directly behind him. Keep a tight lock, not allowing any space between your chest and your partner's back. Start the motion as you extend your back to an upright position. The partner on the bottom should remain in the same position to allow a

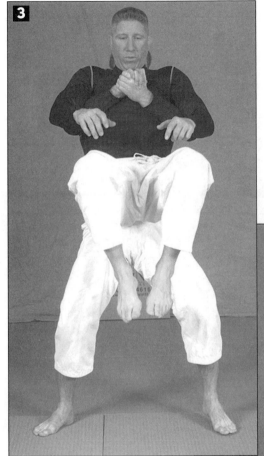

swinging motion on the way back down. This allows for a smooth transition of multiple repetitions.

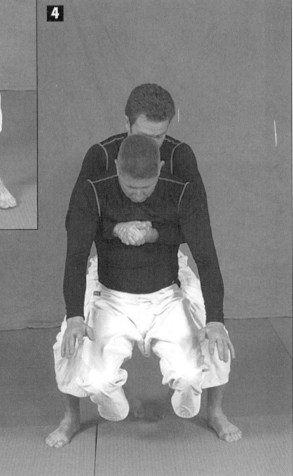

Partner push-ups make working out fun. Simply get into a push-up position facing each other. Do a push at the same time. Once each rep is complete, the partners will shake hands. This makes you balance on one hand as you shake hands. This is a great exercise for kids. This helps develop pushing power as well as core stability and balance.

Partner sit-ups are great exercise for both people; the bottom person will have a great isometric workout just to hold and balance his partner's weight. As the top person does a sit-up, he should be sure not to overextend the back. Do not stretch your back beyond parallel

to the floor. The person on the bottom can get a good neck workout as he assists the sit-up by raising his head during the upward phase of his partner's sit-up.

This illustration shows a very basic drill of movement with extra body weight. With your partner riding piggyback, you will simply make 180-degree turns. This is the same motion your body turns when making a forward throw. This exercise is the same concept of a baseball player who adds weight donuts to

the bat for practice swings. It will result in faster movement once you release the extra weight.

With a group of three, you can get a great workout with this type of exercise. Two people slightly bend over with hands on their knees. The person doing the exercise will do a leapfrog over the first person, then crawl between the legs of the next person. The jumper will come up, turn around, leapfrog over

and crawl under again. This can be repeated as many times as necessary, depending on the goal of your training session.

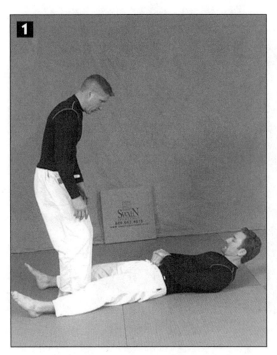

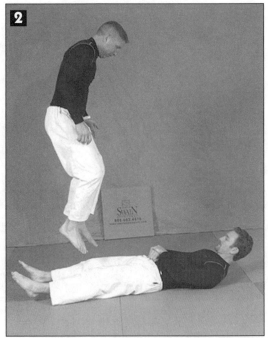

One partner lies on the floor as the other person jumps over his legs. The jumper will alternate landing inside the legs, then outside. The bottom person must continue to open and close his legs at a steady continuous pace. Always jump over the shins and

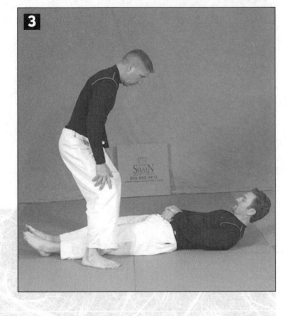

not the feet. Jumping over the feet increases the chances of injury to your partner's ankle if a mistake is made.

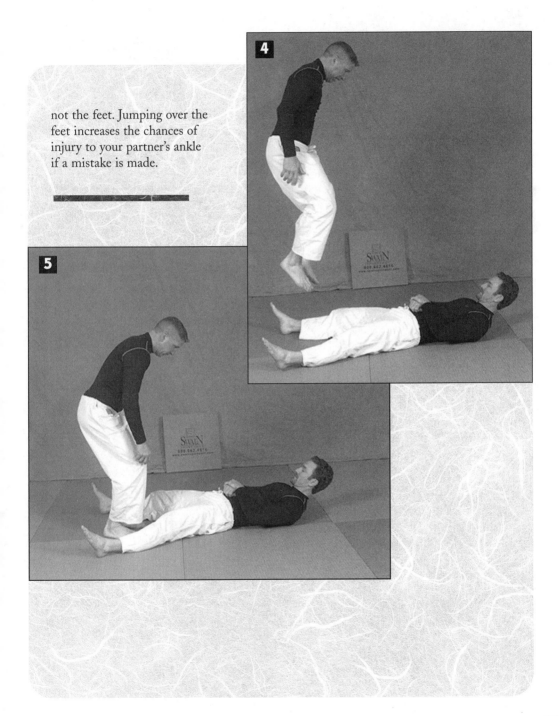

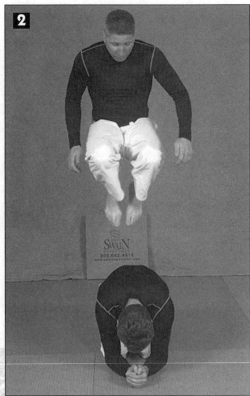

This exercise is a lateral plyometric jump. One person will be on all-fours as the other person will use explosive jumps from one side to the other. This drill will not only increase power and agility, but can also be used for a great conditioning workout.

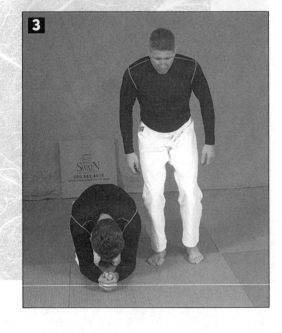

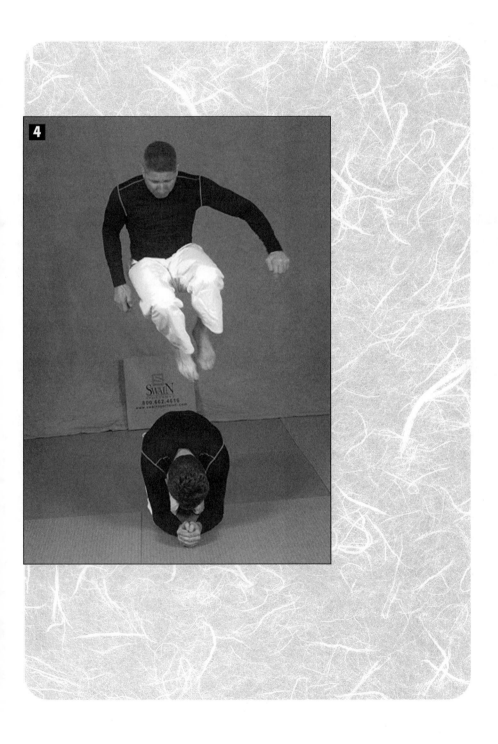

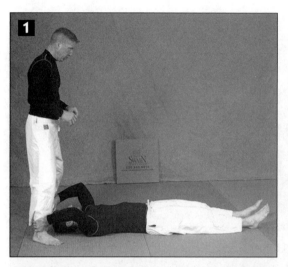

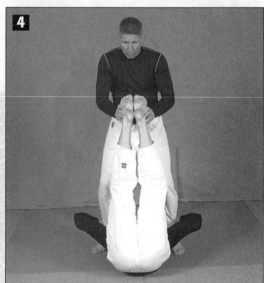

Leg raises are a very important exercise for grappling. Although a partner is not needed to do the basic exercise, using a partner can help increase the intensity. The person on the ground can grab the

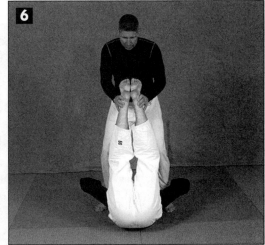

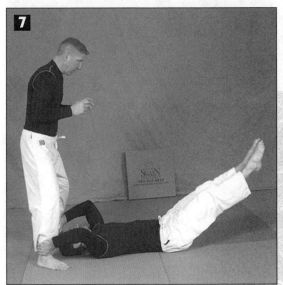

ankles of the standing person for extra stability. As one person raises his legs, the standing person pushes them back down.

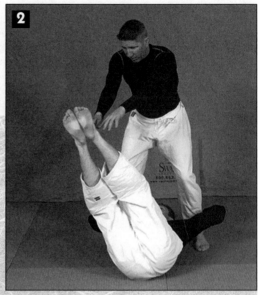

Another variable would be to push not only straight, but push to different angles as well. The exercise is a great workout for the abdominals and hip flexors.

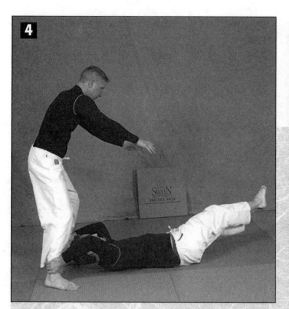

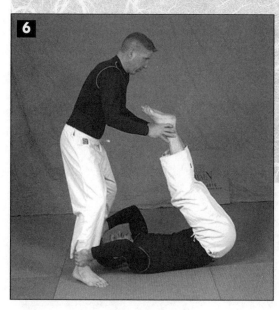

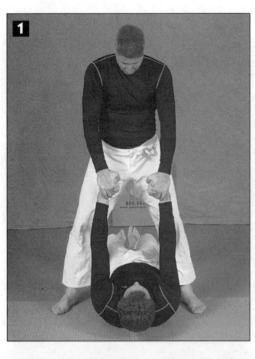

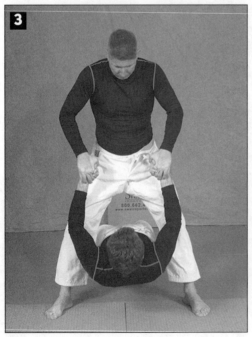

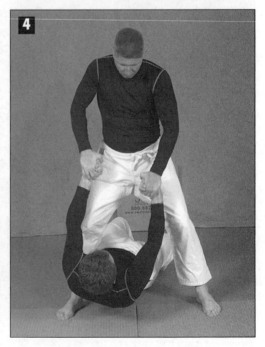

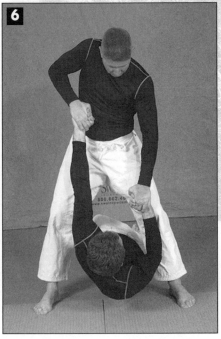

Partner pull-ups can be done by grabbing the hands of a person standing above you. Keep your back rigid as your heels are the only part of your body on the floor. The top person will get a great isometric workout while supporting his partner's weight. An added dimension to this workout would be to alternate pulling hands. This takes more timing, as both partners need to be in sync with each other.

Notes

Notes

Notes

Notes